No One Left Behind

THE REPORT *of the* TWENTIETH
CENTURY FUND TASK FORCE ON
RETRAINING AMERICA'S WORKFORCE

NO ONE LEFT BEHIND

Background Paper by
Carl E. Van Horn

1996 ◆ The Twentieth Century Fund Press ◆ New York

The Twentieth Century Fund sponsors and supervises timely analyses of economic policy, foreign affairs, and domestic political issues. Not-for-profit and nonpartisan, the Fund was founded in 1919 and endowed by Edward A. Filene.

Library of Congress Cataloging-in-Publication Data

Twentieth Century Fund. Task Force on Retraining America's Workforce.
    No one left behind: the report of the Twentieth Century Fund Task Force on Retraining America's Workforce / with background paper by Carl Van Horn.
        p.   cm.
    Includes bibliographical references and index.
    ISBN 0–87078–390–4
    1. Employees--Training of--United States.   2. Occupational retraining--Government policy--United States.   I. Van Horn, Carl E.   II. Title.
    HF5549.5.T7T968   1996
    331.25'924'0973--dc20   96-22571
                                                                                      CIP

Cover Design, Illustration, and Graphics: Claude Goodwin
Manufactured in the United States of America.

FOREWORD

Income stagnation and wealth inequality have become persistent characteristics of our economy. Corporate "downsizing" is a staple of the nightly news. Increasing numbers of workers feel a growing sense of insecurity, believing that they may be the next to lose their jobs regardless of how long they have held them. The result is a great deal of anxiety about the economic future among a majority of Americans.

The question is, Will these economic problems ease, much as past economic woes eventually did? In some respects, history may not be terribly instructive. Today's economic globalization, new technologies, and production innovations, all of which have contributed to greater inequality, are far more pervasive and complex than past developments that might be considered precedents. Other suspected causes of rising inequality and flat earnings, such as declining labor union membership and manufacturing employment, are long-term trends. They may be reversed some day, but they have shown no signs of doing so yet.

Where history may be more useful is the lesson it teaches about education in the United States. Whenever job prospects for the workforce have seemed tenuous, federal, state, and local governments have initiated expensive efforts to provide education and training to more Americans. The G.I. Bill helped veterans returning from the war; spending for elementary and secondary schools increased more than 275 percent in inflation-adjusted dollars between 1952 and 1970; and publicly subsidized college loans and grants enabled college enrollments to increase by more than 125 percent between 1964 and 1980. The evidence is abundant that those investments yielded ample dividends over time for the U.S. economy and, either directly or indirectly, most Americans.

Without question, the nation's schools and universities will need to do an even better job of educating today's children and young adults, for they will face a far more skills-driven workplace. Although that challenge continues to receive abundant attention at all levels of government, the actual task of improving the skills and knowledge of Americans already in the workforce, which holds greater promise for alleviating wage stagnation and economic inequality than most alternatives, inspires little more than lip service. Most workers receive little opportunity on the job to develop skills that might improve their productivity and long-term earnings prospects. Only a few companies, and then mostly large manufacturers, devote real resources to upgrading the abilities of employees at all levels on an ongoing basis. The government's efforts are confined mainly to poorly funded training and job search assistance programs targeted primarily toward "displaced" workers who have lost jobs that will never return. Studies indicate that most of those programs have not been successful.

To date, public and private sector initiatives to train and retrain workers have been about as uneven as the distribution of wealth. While providing a basic education is widely acknowledged to be the responsibility of state and local government, training is deemed an option for employers to pursue at their own discretion. If they determine that training their workers will enhance corporate profitability, basic microeconomics dictates that they will increase their investment in training until the payoff to the bottom line flattens out. Assessing the benefits, however, has been complicated by such things as the justifiable fear that employees will take their newly developed skills elsewhere, wasting the firm's investment.

Government efforts to encourage corporate investments in training have been half-hearted in this period where laissez-faire capitalism has such strong support. Confining government programs mainly to displaced workers avoids some political pitfalls but shrinks the constituency supporting the programs.

Given this situation, politicians of all persuasions, business executives, labor leaders, and educators have formed a rare consensus in support of the notion that the United States needs to invest substantially more money and effort toward improving the skills and knowledge of its workforce. But to date, when anyone asks, "How?" that agreement has unraveled. In search of a consensus, the Twentieth Century Fund convened a Task Force on Retraining America's Workforce. The members of the Task Force—a diverse group of business executives and representatives, union leaders, former government officials, academics, and other highly knowledgeable experts—met five times over the course of a year, including a weekend session in Wilton Park, England to study European training programs; what emerged is reflected in this report.

Carl E. Van Horn, professor of political science at the Eagleton Institute of Politics at Rutgers University, served as executive director of the Task Force and wrote the background paper for the group. James Florio, the former governor of New Jersey whose administration launched a number of training and other economic initiatives, chaired the group. The Fund is grateful to them for their efforts.

Some recent reports, including one released in April by the Clinton administration's Council of Economic Advisers, suggest that corporate downsizing may be leveling off while the rate of job growth is accelerating. And the Labor Department reported in May that wages and salaries increased at a faster pace in the first quarter of 1996 than any time since 1991. But even in that apparently improved economic climate, those same reports acknowledge, earnings disparities continue to be wide.

The Twentieth Century Fund is moving to examine this issue on many fronts at the same time. In addition to this Task Force, we are currently supporting projects looking at various aspects of jobs and the economy; for example, Barry Bluestone and Bennett Harrison are assessing policies for economic growth, James K. Galbraith is examining aspects of wage stagnation, and Edward Wolff is updating his widely read Fund paper exploring wealth inequality, *Top Heavy*.

We thank the members for their time and their commitment to developing recommendations about this critical issue, which is so important to the future of our nation.

RICHARD C. LEONE, *PRESIDENT*
The Twentieth Century Fund
May 1996

CONTENTS

Members of the Task Force

James Florio, *Task Force Chair*
Senior Partner, Florio & Perucci, P.C.

Stephen Blair
President, Career College Association

Anthony P. Carnevale
Vice President for Public Leadership, Educational Testing Service

John D. Correnti
Vice Chairman and Chief Executive Officer, Nucor Corporation

Phyllis Eisen
Senior Policy Director, Human Resources Policy Department,
National Association of Manufacturers

Norman Evans
Visiting Professor in Cooperative Education, Anglia Polytechnic
University, England

William D. Ford
Partner, Patton Boggs, L.L.P.

Ernest Green
Managing Director, Lehman Brothers, and Chairman, African
Development Foundation

Matina S. Horner
Executive Vice President, TIAA-CREF

ROBERTS T. JONES
President and CEO, National Alliance of Business

JOHN A. JORDAN, JR.
Senior Vice President, Bethlehem Steel Corporation

LEWIS B. KADEN
Partner, Davis, Polk & Wardwell

JIMMY P. MORRISON
Executive Vice President, Main Line and Infrastructure Division,
Siemens Transportation Systems

PAUL OSTERMAN
Professor of Human Resources and Management, Sloan School
of Management, Massachusetts Institute of Technology

JANE MCDONALD-PINES
Executive Assistant, Human Resources Development Institute,
AFL-CIO

PAULA REEDER
Education Finance Management and Development Consultant

ROBERT B. SCHWARTZ
Director, Education Program, The Pew Charitable Trusts

JACK SHEINKMAN
Chairman of the Board, Amalgamated Bank of New York

CARL E. VAN HORN, *Task Force Executive Director and
Background Paper Author*
Professor of Public Policy, Eagleton Institute, Rutgers University

DAVID SMITH, *Task Force Consultant*
Fellow, The Twentieth Century Fund

EXECUTIVE SUMMARY

The symptoms of economic insecurity are familiar to most American workers: stagnant earnings, unreliable jobs, shaky employee benefits, and rising income and wealth inequality. Corporate downsizings affecting all kinds of workers—blue and white collar, manufacturing and service sector, executives and front-line employees have become so pervasive even during the current period of economic growth that few Americans consider their jobs to be safe.

Proposed remedies abound for the problems afflicting today's workers. Suggested solutions range from new restrictions on immigration and trade to universal health insurance to penalties against "irresponsible" companies. But to date, little agreement has emerged beyond a general sense that enhancing the education and training of the American workforce probably should be a component of any effort to improve prospects for today's employees. Because workers with greater skills and knowledge are more likely to be prosperous than those without marketable abilities, the basic logic for enabling more Americans to become more productive is compelling.

To develop a specific course of action for upgrading the abilities of the workforce, the Twentieth Century Fund convened a bipartisan Task Force on Worker Retraining comprising representatives of business, labor, government, academia, and others with expertise in the subject. Over the course of the year-long deliberations that included meetings in Wilton Park, England to study European training initiatives, the Task Force reached a consensus: lifelong learning that continuously enhances the skills and knowledge of *all* workers is essential if the benefits of a growing economic

3

pie are to be shared with a larger portion of the population. Widespread lifelong learning would enhance the productivity of the American workforce, launching a cycle of higher U.S. corporate profitability and economic growth that would further benefit American households.

The evidence clearly shows that education and training improves the compensation, job satisfaction, and future career prospects for workers. Companies that invest in improving the skills of their employees also gain because their employees become more productive, which can boost profits. Those mutual benefits of lifelong learning have the potential to help establish a new compact between management and labor, replacing the bonds that have frayed through widespread corporate downsizing. As the catalyst of this new compact, the government's role should be to push both companies and workers to make a commitment to lifelong learning in cooperation with unions and educational institutions.

Of course, primary and secondary education is critical as well. But the vast majority of public and private educational resources are directed toward children and young adults, leaving relatively little for Americans aged twenty-five and over. As many workers have learned the hard way, relying on a high school or even college degree and neglecting to improve one's skills throughout adulthood is a high-stakes gamble.

The Task Force estimates that there is currently a "training gap" of $120 billion: the private sector now spends an estimated $40 billion on formal education and training but would need to invest $160 billion if all companies were to emulate firms that place a high priority on strengthening the abilities of their employees. Bridging that gap will require fundamental changes aimed at developing a culture in which 1) companies habitually strive to enhance the abilities of all their employees, not just top executives; 2) government successfully and efficiently helps the unemployed and workers with little access to training develop skills that are in demand; and 3) workers exert the effort required to improve their value in the job market. The Task Force believes that it would be in the best interest of many companies to follow the example of a host of successful firms that have adopted so-called high-performance strategies, which entail shifting greater responsibility to frontline employees, encouraging teamwork, and providing workers with technological tools and skills that enable them to continuously improve their productivity.

Congress is currently considering legislation to reorganize federal retraining programs, which mainly attempt to serve the unemployed. The Task Force believes that, if enacted, those reforms would be beneficial to the extent that they consolidate and simplify the current federal system. But the legislation could also be counterproductive because the congressional proposals cut funding for future training without taking concrete steps to narrow the $120 billion training gap.

The Task Force believes a far more ambitious and integrated effort is needed, requiring federal and state governments, companies, educational institutions, and workers themselves to devote greater resources and energy toward developing those skills that the labor market values. We do not recommend new governmental training programs because the challenge the nation is facing requires a cooperative partnership in which all participants share burdens and responsibilities; government's role is essential, but it also should be limited mainly to stimulating lifelong learning in the workplace and educational institutions.

Among the Task Force's principal conclusions are the following:

♦ *The federal government should provide a tax credit for companies that increase their investment in educating and training employees.* Many companies do not currently invest much in training, either because they perceive the costs to be too high or because they fear that their employees will take their new skills elsewhere, negating the investment. In search of ways to overcome that resistance to corporate training, the Task Force considered, but rejected, proposals to mandate that companies provide a specified amount of training or face penalties. Such rules would be enormously difficult to administer, would run the risk of bankrupting some companies, and are not likely to change corporate cultures. Instead, the Task Force believes that because training workers is in the best interest of employers, public policies ought to take the form of carrots rather than sticks, and be aimed at helping firms recognize for themselves that they should upgrade the skills of their workers. At the same time, the Task Force decided against recommending that broad training subsidies be provided to all firms, arguing that substituting government funds for private spending that would occur anyway would be wasteful. A tax credit therefore would be the best mechanism for stimulating greater corporate investment in the skills of workers, helping to shrink the training gap. To target the tax credit toward investments that probably would not otherwise be made, the Task Force recommends that the credit apply only after a company's training outlays increase by more than 5 percent above its average over the previous three years. The credit would be worth 35 percent of the excess investment over that level and would likely cost the federal government a little over $1 billion a year.

♦ *The federal government should provide tax deductions to individuals who pay for their own education and training.* Federal and state governments offer substantial support for young people attending colleges and universities on a full-time basis. The combination of grants, loans, and direct subsidies has helped to build the finest and most widely accessible higher education system in the world. But just as policymakers concluded more than thirty years ago that public investment in higher education was necessary for entry-level workers, the Task Force believes that the national interest would be best served by creating mechanisms to encourage and help workers learn throughout their lives. Therefore, the Task Force recommends that the federal government establish a tax deduction to help individuals finance the costs of upgrading their skills. The write-off should be based on the principle of ability to pay, with those making the least income eligible for a more generous deduction than those who earn more. Expenditures that qualify for the credit could finance courses offered by a wide range of post-secondary institutions. Tax deductions would encourage people to invest in education and training, regardless of whether they are employed, even if their employer does not provide benefits for this purpose.

♦ *The federal government should expand eligibility for student financial assistance programs under Title IV of the Higher*

Education Act to assist individuals who enroll in training programs and courses on a less than half-time basis. This reform would enable individuals to qualify for up to $1,500 in Pell grants and/or borrow up to $2,500 under the federal Family Education and Direct Loan Programs to finance their training and education. Loans should be provided only to individuals enrolled in courses of study that will improve their basic educational abilities or upgrade occupational skills.

◆   *The federal-state unemployment insurance system should be reformed to enable those who have lost their jobs to upgrade their skills.* Unemployment insurance helps millions who experience temporary spells of unemployment, but it is not sufficient for those who remain unemployed for longer than the six month cutoff period—one in five workers during the last recession. The Task Force recommends several strategies for connecting unemployment insurance recipients to job search and training assistance without undermining the vital security that the system provides: 1) unemployment insurance recipients most likely to experience long jobless spells should receive early, intensive job search assistance and training building on successful experiments described in the Task Force Report; 2) *all* unemployment insurance recipients, under certain conditions, should be allowed to participate in training without losing their benefits; 3) individuals eligible for unemployment insurance who do not have sufficient cash on hand to pay tuition or training bills, and who are not eligible for student loans, should be permitted to collect up to 30 percent of the unemployment compensation benefits to which they are entitled in a lump sum to help finance the cost of qualified occupational training; and 4) the federal unemployment surcharge of 0.2 percent that is scheduled to expire in 1999 should be retained for strengthening the nation's labor market information network and/or assisting Americans whose unemployment extends beyond six months.

◆   *The federal government should provide vastly improved, integrated, job market information that would be much easier to find and understand.* Although the U.S. Employment Service was established some sixty years ago, its already paltry budget has been diminished, making the United States the only industrialized nation that does not have a strong, publicly funded labor exchange agency as the center of labor market policy. A nationally organized, but decentralized, workforce information system would provide accessible, on-line information about job openings, occupational skills standards, and training and education resources. Good information also is essential to support the training voucher programs outlined in the job training legislation that Congress is considering. Without timely and rich information, individuals may make poor investments with the vouchers the government would provide to pay for training. The Task Force Report includes specific categories of information that should be made available.

◆ *Federal and state governments should help to guarantee private sector training loans to eligible companies.* A majority of firms say they would increase funds spent on training if they had access to working capital loans from banks and other conventional lenders. Small- and medium-sized firms face the greatest reluctance on the part of commercial financial institutions when it comes to obtaining loans for training. The Task Force endorses innovative concepts that create partnerships between government and the private financial sector to increase the availability of private capital for training and retraining the workforce. Several states, including Connecticut, Maryland, and Wisconsin, offer valuable models for providing state-funded loss reserves for private training loan programs offered through participating banks.

◆ *Decisions about awarding government contracts should take into account whether companies who have made bids attempt to develop high performance work organizations and upgrade the skills of their employees.* Investment in workplace education and training would escalate if companies seeking government contracts were required to demonstrate that they invest in improving the skills of their workers. This recommendation would serve as an additional incentive to induce greater private sector training.

◆ *Public-private partnerships created to develop skills stan-*
dards that clarify the abilities employers are looking for and
the qualifications workers must have should focus on those
skills that are of greatest value in a broad array of jobs. Under
the aegis of the National Skills Standards Development Board
(which was authorized by the Goals 2000: Educate America
Act), educators, industrial organizations, and unions are striving to define skill clusters and competencies needed in many
sectors of the economy. The Board hopes these standards will
help businesses improve employee performance, enable educators to better understand the abilities companies seek, and
thereby reduce corporate hiring, selection, and training costs.
Skills standards should also increase the likelihood that potential students will be able to identify education and training
institutions that offer certified programs and that students ultimately will be able to transfer training certificates from one
employer to another to the next. While the Task Force
applauds the efforts of the National Skills Standards project,
there is a danger that it may focus too much on narrow occupational clusters at the expense of skills required in a broader
assortment of jobs. The Task Force urges greater attention to
developing standards for more generic communication, interpersonal, problem-solving, and computer skills, such as those
recommended by the Secretary's Commission on Achieving
Necessary Skills (SCANS).

◆ *Colleges and universities should create workforce develop-*
ment centers that offer technical assistance and support to
companies and unions attempting to institute effective work-
place learning practices. Most community colleges and some
four-year institutions are already playing an important role in
providing vocational skills training for both employed and
unemployed adults. The role of higher education institutions
should be expanded. Workforce development centers modeled
after the successful agricultural extension services that are
found in land-grant colleges and universities should be established to assist employers and unions with education and training
programs for employed or unemployed workers. The centers,
which could be selected through a competitive bidding process

administered by the states, might be funded in part by the federal government with matching grants from the states. They would provide research and information on education and training practices to interested businesses and labor unions; offer in-depth technical assistance and evaluation services to employers, business associations, and unions on a fee-for-service basis; and facilitate and lead the formation of consortia of trade organizations, unions, and businesses to develop and provide training programs through start-up grants and loans.

◆ *Educational institutions that provide job training should be evaluated regularly according to specific standards and performance benchmarks.* The U.S. Secretaries of Education and Labor should work with a broad-based panel of practitioners and experts, including business and labor representatives, to develop detailed standards for public and private employment and training programs. Once adopted, institutions failing to meet these standards should be ineligible to receive public funds directly or indirectly. Private employers should also insist upon adherence to these standards.

* * *

The evidence supporting the potential benefits of training, as well as additional information and positions that the Task Force discussed before reaching its conclusions, are provided in the text of the Report.

Report of the Task Force

For years now, unemployment and inflation in the United States have remained low while the economy has grown. Labor productivity has improved at impressive rates in a wide range of sectors and stock prices have soared to record highs along with corporate profits. Nonetheless, these are not prosperous times for many American workers. Wage increases are barely keeping up with living costs, employee benefits are becoming less secure, and rampant corporate restructuring leaves almost everyone wondering whether a pink slip is in the offing. Although companies that subsidize health insurance and other benefits for their workers have faced higher costs for those outlays, the fact that their employers are paying more is not perceived as a gain by employees. From the standpoint of both income and wealth, the gap between the haves and the have-nots has grown wider than at any time since the Great Depression.

Since the early 1970s, the incomes of 80 percent of the nation's households have not kept up with inflation despite a rising share of dual-income families and even three-job households.[1] Median household incomes fell nearly 5 percent in the last sixteen years after taking inflation into account.[2] In 1979, the median income earner made $496 a week in today's dollars; in 1995, he or she earned $475 a week.

As wages stagnated, the prospect of losing a job that would never return escalated. During the 1980s—a decade of strong economic growth and job creation—over 20 million people lost their jobs permanently.[3] The percentage of jobless Americans who remained unemployed for more than six months jumped from

about 5 percent in 1970 to over 20 percent in 1992.[4] And about
three-quarters of those laid off in 1992 and 1993 did not expect to
return to their jobs, the highest levels since such data was first collected in 1967.[5] More than half of the Fortune 500 manufacturing
companies have reduced their workforces since 1989 and every
last one of those 500 predicted that they would downsize in the
next five years.[6]

Millions of permanent and full-time jobs have been replaced by
temporary or part-time positions, giving rise to what has become
known as the contingent workforce. Temporary jobs, which may
be full-time positions, now represent 6 percent of jobs available
to the labor force and the number is growing rapidly.[7] During the
1980s, the temporary help industry grew ten times faster than overall employment.[8] Part-time jobs have been the source of much of
the job growth since the 1970s, but most of those working part-
time would rather be in full-time jobs.[9]

An array of factors has been blamed for the travails of the
American worker: increased foreign trade and business competition, technological changes such as the influx of computers into
work places, declining membership in labor unions, shrinking
employment in manufacturing, corporate consolidation, new systems for organizing work, and immigration. To varying degrees, all
of those forces have contributed to the economic anxiety that has
become pervasive in the United States. But those fundamental structural changes are unlikely suddenly to reverse course.

Because little consensus has yet emerged about the most
promising route toward improving earnings prospects and strengthening job security for American workers, the Twentieth Century
Fund convened a Task Force on Worker Retraining to consider
what actions ought to be pursued. The Task Force focused on ideas
intended to help those already in the workforce, including the long-
term unemployed. It did not deliberate over reform of the primary and secondary educational systems, which have been the subject
of abundant attention. Nor did the Task Force delve into broader
economic issues like fiscal, job creation, monetary, trade, and social
policies.

The central conclusion of the Task Force is that improving
living standards and relieving economic anxiety requires strengthening the education and training of Americans in the workforce as

well as "dislocated" workers who have lost jobs that will never return. The Task Force believes that lifelong learning that continuously upgrades the skills and knowledge of all workers, including those without jobs, offers the best hope for sharing the benefits of a growing economic pie with a larger portion of the population. Relying on a high school diploma or a college degree and failing to acquire additional abilities after entering the workforce is a high-stakes gamble that has cost millions of Americans dearly.

Most current governmental and corporate workforce training programs and practices in the United States were fashioned in an environment that has disappeared. These policies were well suited to a labor market where the knowledge and skills gained in school prior to entering the workforce were sufficient to sustain people for their entire working lives. But the entrenched pattern of providing schooling into early adulthood followed by minimal learning on the job is not sufficient in today's economy. While the Task Force endorses efforts to reform primary and secondary education as well as initiatives to smooth the school-to-work transition, we believe that much greater effort is needed to help working Americans to improve their skills. More reliable and useful information about job openings and employer needs, vastly improved job training and educational services, and stronger incentives to promote employer investments in training while inducing workers to help themselves are all essential. To that end, new partnerships among business, unions, government, schools, professional associations, and individuals will be needed to transform good ideas into productive action.

The Task Force believes that lifelong learning is essential to improving the prospects for the American worker because all evidence suggests that in today's economy, those who receive the most training and education are the most likely to prosper. A recent study by the Organization for Economic Cooperation and Development shows that the gap in wages between rich and poor is wider in the United States than in any other industrialized nation, with educational level the most important factor in determining who wins and who loses.[10]

In the United States, college-educated workers are the only segment of the population whose wages have not fallen in this decade after taking inflation into account.[11] Women who attended or graduated from college increased their earnings by 16 percent; whereas men with only a high school education experienced a 14 percent cut in earnings and high school dropouts lost 22.5 percent, after adjusting for inflation.[12]

Education and training have always affected lifetime earnings, but better educated and trained workers are even more likely to get ahead in today's labor market. In 1979, college graduates' average hourly wage was $15.22, whereas high school graduates earned $11.23—a difference of 38 percent. In 1993, the average wage of college graduates had increased to $15.71, but high school graduates' average hourly wage dropped to $9.92—a gap of 58 percent.[13]

Economists have demonstrated that learning in school and on the job accounts for a great deal of the differences in earnings among Americans. Several studies have demonstrated that receiving company-sponsored formal training has significant positive effects on the earnings of employees.[14] People who receive such formal education or training on the job have a 30 percent earnings advantage over those who do not.[15] Unfortunately, no more than a third of Americans participate in formal education or training after they leave high school or college.[16]

For many decades, the United States has spent a higher proportion of its gross domestic product on elementary, secondary, and higher education than any other industrialized nation. In 1993, for example, the United States spent $24,300 per capita on education, versus $20,500 in Japan, $18,700 in France, $18,500 in Germany, and $17,000 in the United Kingdom.[17] A higher percentage of U.S. high school graduates enrolls in post-secondary educational programs than do any other country's graduates.[18] There is evidence, however, that these investments have not always paid off in academic performance. In nearly every international comparison in mathematics and science, for example, U.S. students perform less well than students from other advanced industrial nations.[19] Moreover, our economic counterparts spend more on and do a better job of upgrading the skills of workers after they join the workforce. The typical European or Japanese company places greater value on learning on the job and is more likely to use education to reward employees.[20] Both the public and private sectors in Western Europe invest heavily to enhance the skills of their workers.[21] The European Union is implementing comprehensive labor market policies that will substantially increase public and private investments in training, including a commitment to universal advanced vocational training and the right to training throughout one's lifetime.[22]

Policies promoting human capital development beyond the school years are reflected in government budgets. The U.S. government spends a smaller percentage of the U.S. gross domestic product (GDP) on improving the skills of adult workers than any industrialized nation except Japan, where employer-based training is deeply ingrained in workplace cultures.[23] Although part of the gap in training investment is explained by the higher structural unemployment levels in Europe, it also reflects profound differences in spending priorities. In 1994, the American government spent less than .25 percent of gross domestic product helping employed and unemployed citizens improve their job skills. In contrast, the German government spent 2 percent of its GDP and France 1 percent of its GDP on training and retraining programs.[24]

Creating new opportunities for working Americans to develop skills day-in and day-out will require an enormous effort on the part of employers, federal, state, and local governments; educational and training institutions; unions; and workers themselves. Current congressional efforts to reorganize federal retraining programs will help in some respects and hurt in others. But pending legislation falls far short of the fundamental changes necessary to develop a culture in which 1) companies habitually strive to enhance the abilities of all their employees, 2) government successfully and efficiently helps the unemployed and workers with little access to training to develop skills in demand, and 3) workers exert the effort required to improve their value in the job market.

CORPORATE INVESTMENTS IN WORKERS

Various studies have estimated that private employers spend over $40 billion annually on training their workers, or a little over 1 percent of their payroll.[25] But the Task Force believes this seemingly sizable investment is far from adequate. Only 10 percent of American workers receive any formal training from employers aimed at upgrading their job skills, although that percentage seems to be growing and much informal training is not measured in most analyses of private firms. Ninety percent of the training dollars that are accounted for are spent by less than 1 percent of U.S. firms, or about 15,000 companies.[26] The lion's share of corporate training is devoted to improving the performance of white-collar executives, technicians, and other already well-educated workers, while lower echelon employees typically receive little if any training. [27]

There are indications that training practices may be spreading as more manufacturing firms adopt principles of "high performance workplaces," endorsed by management and labor, that emphasize the importance of training and giving responsibility to frontline workers. Joint union-management training agreements involving the United Auto Workers, the United Steel Workers, the Service Employees Union, the Building and Construction Trade Unions, the Amalgamated Clothing and Textile Workers Union (now UNITE, the Union of Needletrades, Industrial, and Textile Employees)[28] all include formal labor-management commitments to upgrade the skills of workers at most job levels in order to enhance both worker productivity and job security. The challenge, in the view of the Task Force, is to find ways to encourage more firms to emulate such efforts at integrating training strategies for employees throughout the country.

Fully recognizing the value of human resources to corporate performance requires companies to make cultural changes that include, but are not limited to, greater investment in training. The operational design of workplaces—the degree of responsibility given to workers, the ways in which they are encouraged to interact with one another and with counterparts outside the firm, the technological resources available to them, and so forth—contributes in fundamental ways to the development of employee skills that can improve the bottom line. The skills of greatest value to any given company will depend on that operational design of its workplace, its strategic business plan, and the existing skills of its workers. Those factors, in turn, will influence how skills might be developed, whether through on-the-job training, changing work assignments, or "performance support systems" that induce workers to develop their own ideas for improving productivity. The nature of the more formalized training that a company might provide—skill modules, job-specific instruction, just-in-time inventory training—also will depend on the company's particular circumstances. Throughout the corporate landscape, firms that demonstrate that they highly value their employees through the way in which they organize their workplaces and support skill improvements are prospering. The cultural changes required can be wrenching, but steadfast executives who placed their faith in upgrading their human resources are reaping abundant benefits.[29]

Despite such promising initiatives, too much evidence suggests that the basic literacy and technical skills of American workers are deficient. The National Center for Education Statistics estimates that about 40 million people in the workplace have difficulty reading and writing. Four in ten U.S. business executives complain they cannot modernize equipment to compete more effectively because their workers do not have the appropriate skills.[30] A survey of Fortune 1000 executives by the Opinion Research Corporation found that 90 percent claimed that these basic literacy and skill problems in the workforce affected corporate productivity and profitability.

Not enough firms have acted on Task Force member Anthony Carnevale's observation that, "The competitive advantage of developed nations lies in the application of technological advances in combination with an increasingly skilled and adaptable work force."[31] Some of the nation's most successful global firms, however, have heard that message. These companies, such as Motorola, Hewlett-Packard, Microsoft, and NYNEX, typically spend more than 4 percent of payroll on training programs for frontline workers—nearly three times the national average.[32] Most successful high technology firms emphasize learning on the job to meet the demands of technological change and world competition. They conduct performance reviews of individual training and education needs and develop customized strategies for each employee, while paying for the costs of educating and training their workers.[33] And more than $500 million is spent on training through joint labor-management apprenticeship programs in the building and construction trades.

So if workplace learning is so important, why don't companies devote more resources to it? Many companies fear that they won't benefit from investing in their employees' skills because those workers might take those new abilities with them to another firm—

perhaps even a competitor. Since a great deal of employer-provided training improves generic communication, problem solving, and computer skills that most companies covet in their workers, corporate concern about failing to reap the benefits of training is understandable. Corporate education and training is expensive, especially during the start-up phases. And the payoff to the bottom line has not always been well documented. High costs and uncertainty about payoffs may deter small- and medium-sized firms that cannot spread the fixed costs of training. Most firms have not been able to convince those in financial centers of the connection between training and higher profits.[34]

Yet in the computer software industry, where workers are more likely to move among competing firms, companies nonetheless invest heavily in training because a firm that fails to do so would be less likely to continue creating state-of-the-art products. As companies in older industries recognize that the competitive advantages of training may outweigh the risks of losing some workers, practices in the software industry ought to become more common elsewhere.[35]

Indeed, there is mounting evidence that human capital investments pay off for the firm and not just for the individual. The Task Force reviewed the evidence about the impact of company-sponsored education and training and heard testimony from its members. The Task Force concluded that the combination of high performance work systems and high levels of training produce substantial returns on investments, increased productivity, and higher quality products and services. The key is increasing worker participation in the process of workplace reform.

After reviewing a large body of research, Rosemary Batt and Task Force member Paul Osterman concluded that "[1] education and training are associated with significant productivity increases . . . and [2] training and associated flexible human resources systems are associated with higher levels of productivity and quality in matched comparisons."[36] Consider the following studies:

◆   A National Association of Manufacturers report found that companies with high-performance practices, such as employee involvement in decisionmaking and compensation linked to worker performance and training, had higher productivity, higher morale, decreased workers' compensation costs, lower absenteeism, and reduced defect rates.[37]

◆   A study of seventy-two small- and medium-sized firms revealed moderate to significant positive impacts from firm-sponsored education programs on worker morale, communications abilities, company loyalty, reading ability, and quality of output.[38]

◆   An investigation of training strategies in 155 manufacturing firms concluded that those with formal training programs had higher productivity growth rates than firms that did not have training programs. Firms beginning with productivity levels below the industry average brought their productivity levels up to industry standards in three years after the introduction of formal training programs.[39]

◆   A number of studies have found that union involvement in workplace transformation programs significantly improved labor productivity, product quality, labor-management relations, as well as job satisfaction and employment security.[40]

In summary, the Task Force believes that it is in the best interest of most companies to invest far more substantially than they now do in the skills of their employees on an ongoing basis. But because many firms will continue to resist making such efforts due to their fear that trained workers will take their skills elsewhere and because of the high costs associated with initiating new training strategies, the Task Force also maintains that far more aggressive government action is needed to increase opportunities for lifelong learning.

GOVERNMENTAL INVESTMENT IN WORKERS

Federal, state, and local policymakers have paid relatively little attention to the education and training of Americans in the workforce. Between 80 percent and 90 percent of the nearly $500 billion annually spent on education and training in the United States is allocated to primary, secondary, and higher education.[41] Over the last decade, most states have reformed public school curricula and imposed tougher graduation standards. And within the last two years, Congress passed laws establishing national goals for educational reform and nationwide programs to help students make the transition from school to work. Improving the nation's basic, entry-level workforce preparation system is a vital task—one that will take years to complete. Moreover, it will require a shift in priorities so that students who are not college bound receive more assistance in their post-high school years.

The Task Force applauds these efforts at school reform. But because more than 75 percent of those who will be working in the year 2000 are already out of school, much greater effort also needs to be exerted toward improving the skills of those already in the job market in order to help enhance the economic well-being of workers and alleviate their anxiety about remaining employed. Today, more than 90 percent of the federal government's spending on the workforce is directed toward insurance payments for the temporarily unemployed, which is intended primarily to serve as income support to tide workers over from one job to the next. The remaining money goes toward an array of programs that provide training and job placement assistance for some workers who have permanently lost their jobs or who face other economic hardship. Although Congress is expected to consolidate most of these training programs, the Task Force believes that current federal and state government efforts are insufficient and poorly suited to promoting lifelong learning.

An overview of those programs:

RETRAINING WORKERS ON THE JOB. The federal government provides only minimal incentives for companies to invest in their employees and for workers to invest in themselves. Like most corporate costs, companies can deduct training outlays from their revenues in computing their income taxes. Workers who pay for their own training and education can deduct the expense on their tax returns only if the classes relate directly to their current jobs.

A small but growing number of states provide assistance to firms that are willing to retrain their workers rather than lay them off. In fiscal year 1994, seventeen states spent approximately $380 million on workforce adjustment programs that included support for those at risk of unemployment.[42] Few formal assessments of the success of those efforts have been conducted, but anecdotal evidence is encouraging. For example, 13,500 individuals at risk of job termination who were enrolled in California's employer-based training programs increased their earnings by $4,500, or 15 percent, in the year after training. Previously unemployed workers who completed similar training increased their earnings by $10,000, or 88 percent, within a year after finishing their training. In the year following retraining, these participants experienced fewer weeks of unemployment and received less unemployment compensation than those who dropped out. Income gains persisted two years after completing the program.[43]

ASSISTING THE LONG-TERM UNEMPLOYED. Unemployment insurance, by far the largest program, provides temporary and partial income replacement for people while they wait to return to their previous employers or seek new jobs. The federal and state governments both levy taxes on employers, and the federal government holds the revenues in a trust fund for distribution to the states as needed. The U.S. government determines the system's basic rules, but the states have considerable leeway in specifying eligibility for assistance, benefit levels, and duration. In fiscal year 1994, payments amounted to $31 billion—nearly the same amount spent on Aid to Families with Dependent Children (AFDC).

Unemployment insurance was designed in the 1930s to cope with temporary layoffs arising from economic recessions. But because three-quarters of today's jobless do not expect to return to their previous employer, the program is no longer suited to the needs of many of the unemployed. The income support helps the unemployed pay for basic needs, but it does not produce more highly skilled workers or more competitive industries because it does not encourage workers or companies to invest in human capital. In fact, in most states, the unemployed risk losing their UI benefits if they enroll in training and education programs.

The federal government also funds several other less costly programs for the long-term unemployed, many of which are part of Title III of the Job Training Partnership Act (JTPA). Those programs provide additional income maintenance, job search assistance, and retraining to "dislocated" workers—those who have permanently lost their jobs due to the decline of particular industries, international trade, or other specific factors. Still, only 6 percent of workers who have exhausted their unemployment compensation benefits receive job search assistance and only 1.4 percent enroll in federal training programs.[44]

In some cases, the job search assistance efforts have reduced the length of unemployment when used in conjunction with "worker profiling"—a process that uses demographic and work history information to identify individuals who are least likely to obtain a job on their own. When individuals deemed to be "at risk" received intensive job search assistance and counseling, they obtained jobs providing compensation comparable to their previous employment more quickly than those not enrolled. These job search programs are cost effective because the administrative costs are more than offset by the reduced payout period for unemployment compensation and increased tax revenues from the earlier return to work.[45]

In contrast, short-term skills training for long-term unemployed workers has not proven to be successful, either in reducing unemployment duration or in helping individuals restore their previous incomes. Longer-term training programs appear to be more likely to yield favorable results, but the evidence remains inconclusive.[46] JTPA programs favor short-term training programs, and unemployment insurance rules preclude many workers from enrolling in long-term training. Because federal programs for the long-term unemployed have not been coordinated, many workers and employers find them confusing and inaccessible.

EMPLOYMENT AND TRAINING REFORM

Congress is currently considering bills to reform portions of the employment and training system for youth, disadvantaged adults, and the long-term unemployed. If passed by Congress and signed by the president, the legislation would be the first major overhaul of employment and training programs in more than a decade. Although the legislation has not taken final form, enough is known about its basic components for the Task Force to comment on its strengths and weaknesses.

The Senate and House bills would consolidate nearly one hundred employment and training programs into lump-sum block grants, with few strings attached, to the states and local entities. The Senate bill creates one block grant with funding for employment programs (25 percent), education (25 percent), and so-called flexible funds (50 percent) that could be used for any combination of additional employment programs, education, or retraining workers currently in jobs. The House bill establishes four separate block grants with funding for youth, disadvantaged adults, and literacy education. Ten percent of the funds can be transferred from one block grant account to another. The House bill also requires states to make vouchers available through local organizations to individuals seeking education and training services. The Senate bill encourages, but does not require, vouchers. Federal programs would be retained for the Job Corps, provision of labor market information, and workers who lose their jobs in mass layoffs or plant closings.

Under both bills, the block would be distributed first to the states and then to local labor market areas according to federally set allocation formulas. Funds for the labor-exchange services (which provide information about job openings) that state employment service agencies provide would remain under the control of governors and dedicated to those functions, but could be provided through the one-stop career centers or other options that states may choose. The House bill requires states to permit initial registration for unemployment compensation in the same offices in which beneficiaries could also receive local level job placement and training services. The one-stop centers would be governed by oversight boards under private sector leadership, and state and local offices would be obligated to provide detailed performance reports on their efforts. In addition, the House bill, but not the Senate's, establishes consumer "report cards" on education and training institutions and requires that service providers who wish to cash vouchers be certified as meeting student loan criteria or industry-recognized skills standards. Because data collection requirements are quite general, the new job training block grant may produce fifty different measurement systems—making comparisons of performance difficult if not impossible.

POSITIVE ASPECTS OF THE REFORM LEGISLATION. Merging overlapping programs to simplify and improve the accessibility of employment and training services is a long-overdue and welcome step that should be more useful to both the unemployed workers and companies with openings. Giving greater flexibility to the states and localities to administer those services as they see fit should improve their responsiveness to changing local economic conditions. That new flexibility, enhanced by vouchers, may encourage state and local policymakers to create fruitful new partnerships between private firms and workers while tightening the accountability of service providers. In addition, the new laws should improve the availability of higher quality job search assistance for the unemployed, mainly because both bills make a strong commitment to upgrading the quality of labor market information.

EXPANDING THE REFORM AGENDA. Although the employment and training legislation pending in Congress is sensible in many respects, it does not address important issues that concern the Task Force. First, federal authorization for funding employment and training programs would be cut by 15 percent to 20 percent at a time when the number of long-term unemployed adults and youths at risk of unemployment are increasing. Even though the new system might well turn out to be more efficient, any savings are unlikely to outweigh the depletion in direct federal dollars allocated for services intended to help the most vulnerable members of the workforce.

The impact of budget reductions for job training services is likely to be exacerbated by cuts in welfare spending. Welfare reform legislation under consideration would require enrolling up to 50 percent of welfare recipients in job training or related programs and threatens to swamp the newly restructured state and local agencies from the outset. If most job training resources are to be diverted to "welfare-to-work" efforts, then little will be left for other unemployed Americans who are already accustomed to working but need additional training to obtain another decent job.

Second, additional legislation will be needed to encourage companies and workers to invest in improving employee skills. The only aspect of the reforms that are truly geared toward improving the training of employed workers is the provision in the Senate bill allowing flexible spending accounts to be allocated for training if the state establishes state and local private sector oversight boards. But, because the needs of the long-term unemployed, welfare recipients, and disadvantaged youths are likely to be viewed as greater priorities in light of funding cutbacks in programs serving those groups, states may have little choice but to apply most of the flexible account money toward the long-term unemployed. Still, even if all the flexible funds were to be invested in improving the skills of those who are currently employed, the resources would be paltry compared to the needs that the Task Force perceives.

Finally, the bills do not reform unemployment insurance, other than to encourage those registering for it to take advantage of job search services that may be more readily available from the same state or local agency. Under current law, unemployed workers are obliged to search for a job, but they are not required to seek training that might improve their chances of finding one. The new statute would not change expectations for the unemployed, nor give any assistance to those who may want to enroll in further education and training during periods of unemployment.

In summary, the new legislation that is working its way through Congress lacks both the resources and the comprehensiveness needed to promote a new culture oriented toward lifelong learning. Nevertheless, it provides a new foundation on which a more promising and comprehensive effort might be built.

A New Compact for Lifelong Learning

In the post-World War II era, most American workers believed that they could expect lifetime employment in exchange for hard work and loyalty to their employers. Although they might be laid off during economic downturns, they would be called back to their former employers when business recovered. Now that uncontrollable economic forces have obliterated that once sacrosanct compact, the Task Force believes that the mutual benefits of lifelong learning can be the basis for a new relationship between companies and their workers. Firms that invest in the skills of their employees will be rewarded with higher labor productivity and, in all probability, healthier profits; workers who capitalize on opportunities to learn valued skills will benefit from heightened job security and, in all probability, earn higher compensation. As the catalyst of this new compact, the government's role should be to push both companies and workers to make a commitment to lifelong learning in cooperation with unions and educational institutions.

1. Encouraging Employers to Invest in the Skills of Workers

The Task Force considered, but rejected, proposals to mandate that companies provide a specified amount of training or penalize those that do not. Such rules would be enormously difficult to administer, would run the risk of bankrupting some companies, and are not likely to change corporate cultures. Instead, the Task Force believes that because training workers is in the best interest of employers, public policies ought to take the form of carrots rather than sticks to help firms recognize for themselves that they should upgrade the skills of their workers. At the same time, the Task Force decided against providing broad training subsidies to all firms because substituting government funds for private spending that would have occurred anyway would be wasteful.

Recommendations

+ *The federal government, the states, private companies, and U.S. workers all need to devote greater resources and effort toward improving skills that the labor market values throughout each American's career.* Educational investment in the United States has long been concentrated on the early years of life. The evidence is clear that a new mindset oriented toward lifelong learning that continues from a worker's first job through retirement is probably a worker's best hope for enjoying rising living standards and employment security. Private U.S. employers now spend approximately $40 billion annually, or about 1 percent of the nation's total payroll, on educating and training their workers. Most companies do not provide any formal training for their employees, however. In contrast, many highly successful companies invest more than 4 percent of their payroll explicitly on upgrading the skills of their employees. That 4 percent benchmark should be the goal for all firms.

If U.S. companies collectively allocated the equivalent of 4 percent of payroll toward educating and training their workers, the investment would increase from today's $40 billion to about $160 billion annually. To help bridge that $120 billion training gap, the Task Force recommends the specific strategies advocated in this report to stimulate life-long learning. Those strategies will require the government, the private sector, unions, and workers to share a greater financial investment and active commitment toward achieving that goal.

◆ *The federal government should provide a modest tax credit for companies that increase their investment in educating and training employees.* The Task Force believes that the tax incentive would stimulate greater corporate investment in the skills of their workers, helping to shrink the training gap. Direct non-wage expenditures on formal training for frontline workers and supervisors, including expanded tuition assistance, would be counted toward the tax break. To target the credit toward new investments that probably would not otherwise occur, the Task Force recommends that it apply only after a company's training outlays increase by more than 5 percent above its average over the previous three years. The credit would be worth 35 percent of the excess investment over that level.

The proposed tax credit, or a variation of it, would not explode the federal budget deficit. If the credit succeeded in increasing corporate training outlays by 10 percent annually, the cost to the federal government would be about $1.4 billion a year. The Task Force believes that the payoff to companies, workers, and the government itself would far exceed the investment.

Unfortunately, the tax credit is unlikely to encourage small companies to increase their training investments because most such firms do not have sizable tax liabilities. Federal, state, and local governments can help to encourage smaller companies to pool their limited resources and form consortia for small firm training, however. The Task Force endorses initiatives by the National Alliance of Business to support such organizations.[47]

◆   *The federal government should provide vastly improved, inte-
    grated, job market information that would be much easier
    to find and understand.* A crucial resource for workers facing
    a career or job change is good information about job openings,
    educational alternatives, the skills in high demand, and indus-
    try trends. Better informed decisions increase the efficiency
    and flexibility of labor markets, while raising the returns to
    private investments in human capital. But the workforce infor-
    mation systems in the United States must be significantly
    upgraded to be useful for workers and employers. Good infor-
    mation also is essential to support the voucher programs out-
    lined in the new job training legislation. The concept of
    vouchers for training is appealing because it could empower
    individuals to take control of their economic futures. But with-
    out timely and rich information, individuals may make poor
    investments with their vouchers.

    Although the U.S. Employment Service was established
    some sixty years ago, its diminished and paltry budget has
    made the United States the only industrialized nation that does
    not have a strong publicly funded labor exchange agency as
    the center of labor market policy. A nationally organized, but
    decentralized workforce information system would provide
    accessible, on-line information about job openings, occupa-
    tional skills standards, and training and education resources.
    Three principal categories of information should be available:

▲   labor market information based on quarterly wage records
    that show the volume of job openings by area, industry,
    occupation, and wage rates;

▲   descriptions of duties and skill requirements associated
    with job openings;

▲   information about education, employment, and training
    service institutions, including program completion and job
    placement rates, along with potential sources of public sup-
    port for individuals enrolled in education and training
    activities.

The Task Force is encouraged that the reform legislation under consideration by Congress supports these principles, but it regrets that those proposals emphasize state rather than federal responsibilities in providing information about job openings. Because the most attractive job opportunities for workers may be outside the state they currently reside in, the federal government must play an active role in gathering and distributing employment information. Without federal direction and coordination, job market information is less likely to be consistent, uniform, and useful to workers.

Congress probably will set aside only a small portion of the newly authorized job training funds to develop better labor market information. The Task Force believes that a more ambitious revitalization of the U.S. Employment Service and a concerted effort to make better use of labor market information already collected through the unemployment insurance system is essential.

- ◆ *Federal and state governments should help to guarantee private sector training loans to eligible companies.* A majority of firms say they would increase funds spent on training if they had access to working capital loans from banks and other conventional lenders. Small- and medium-sized firms face the greatest reluctance from commercial financial institutions to provide loans for training.[48] The Task Force endorses innovative concepts that create partnerships between government and the private financial sector to increase the availability of private capital for training and retraining the workforce. The efforts of several states, including Connecticut, Maryland, and Wisconsin, to provide state-funded loss reserves for private training loan programs offered through participating banks provide models worthy of widespread replication. Under the legislation moving through Congress, governors would be allowed to set aside a portion of federal block grant resources to provide loan guarantees or loss reserves. Although these programs are still experimental and small in scope, the Task Force urges governors to exercise this option if it is included in the new law.

◆ *The federal and state governments should support customized*
   training programs intended to educate and train workers who
   face a high risk of dislocation. The success of California's
   employer-based training program for workers in danger of permanent layoffs demonstrates that it is worthy of more widespread emulation. To help guard against using public funds on
   private sector efforts that would have taken place anyway, the
   Task Force recommends that most money devoted to these
   activities be concentrated on such start-up costs as assessing
   worker skills and curriculum development. The activities should
   also provide education and training in generic, transferable
   skills that are in demand in many realms of the labor market.[49]
   Because developing new training strategies is expensive, government subsidization of private firms that create workplace
   training programs that can be used by other employers is essential. Federal and state matching grants would be one possible
   mechanism for supporting such private sector investments.

◆ *The awarding of government contracts should take into*
   account whether bidding companies attempt to develop high
   performance work organizations and upgrade the skills of
   their employees. Investment in workplace education and training would escalate if companies seeking government contracts
   were required to demonstrate that they invest in improving
   the skills of their workers. This recommendation would serve
   as an additional "carrot" to induce greater private sector training. Training investments could be included in government
   bids both to improve the product and the firm's workforce.
   The Department of Defense has used this technique for many
   years on technical bids and even requires skills certification
   for individuals performing certain tasks.

2. ENCOURAGING PUBLIC-PRIVATE PARTNERSHIPS THAT WOULD MAKE THE LABOR MARKET MORE EFFICIENT

Most workers have little idea what skills employers value
most, let alone how they should go about attaining those skills.
Without a clear understanding of where the good jobs are, what
skills those jobs require, and where to acquire them, many work-

ers are understandably frustrated at their failure to improve their earnings prospects. Better informing workers about what the job market expects will require extensive collaboration among all levels of government, industry associations, labor unions and organizations, and educational institutions.

RECOMMENDATIONS

- *Public-private partnerships to develop skills standards that clarify the abilities employers seek and the qualifications workers must meet should focus on skills valued in a broad array of jobs.* Under the aegis of the National Skill Standards Board (which was authorized by the Goals 2000: Educate America Act), educators, industrial organizations, and unions are striving to define skill clusters and competencies needed in many sectors of the economy.[50] The Board hopes these standards will help businesses improve employee performance, enable educators to better understand the abilities companies seek, and thereby reduce corporate hiring, selection, and training costs. Skills standards should also increase the likelihood that potential students will be able to identify education and training institutions that offer certified programs and that they ultimately will be able to transfer training certificates from one employer to another to the next.

  While the Task Force applauds the efforts of the national Skills Standards project, there is a danger that it may focus too much on narrow occupational clusters at the expense of skills required in a broader assortment of jobs. Great Britain's analogous National Vocational Qualifications system, which took several years to develop, has been criticized by employers who say the qualifications standards are too narrowly defined for the flexible workforce needs of the future. The Task Force urges greater attention to developing standards for more generic communication, interpersonal, problem solving, and computer skills, such as those recommended by the Secretary's Commission on Achieving Necessary Skills (SCANS).

- *Educational institutions that provide job training should have their effectiveness measured regularly according to specific standards and performance benchmarks. The states and the federal government should report on these measurements.* The U.S. secretaries of education and labor should work with a broad-based panel of practitioners and experts, including business and labor representatives, to develop detailed standards for public and private employment and training programs. Those standards would build on those already established by the International Standards Organization 9000 board. Once adopted, institutions failing to meet these standards should be ineligible to receive public funds, directly or indirectly. Private employers should also insist upon adherence to these standards. The panel should focus on six essential issues:

1. Education and training institutions must work closely with employers and unions to define knowledge, skills, and abilities for particular training programs or courses of study when establishing graduation requirements. The weak connections between education and training institutions, unions, and the nation's businesses must be strengthened.[51]

2. Education and training institutions should more effectively prepare workers to develop essential skills. Today, there are no widely accepted standards for either entry-level or advanced skills in most occupations. The adoption of skill standards by the electronics and retail industries, as well as joint labor-management apprenticeship programs, are encouraging exceptions.

3. In assessing performance, standards should be based on demonstrated proficiencies rather than hours spent in programs.

4. Education and training institutions must adapt their teaching methods and curriculums to meet the needs of older learners.

5. Potential users of education and training services—employers, unions, and individuals—must receive accurate and comprehensive information on the results of specific programs

and institutions, including completion rates, placements, job retention, and wages obtained by program graduates. Today, by and large, reporting requirements are limited and uninformative.

6. The National Skill Standards Board, the American National Standards Initiative, or the American Society of Quality Control could accept responsibility for the tasks outlined above and develop standards for evaluating training institutions and programs.

♦ *Colleges and universities should create workforce development centers offering technical assistance and support to companies and unions attempting to institute effective workplace learning practices.* Most community colleges, private career colleges and schools, and some four-year institutions are already playing an important role in providing vocational skills training for both employed and unemployed adults.[52] The role of institutions that provide higher education should be expanded.

Modeled after the successful agricultural extension services that are found in land-grant colleges and universities, workforce development centers should be established to assist employers and unions with education and training programs for workers (employed or unemployed).[53] The centers, which could be selected after a competitive bidding process administered by the states, might be funded in part by the federal government with matching grants from the states. The centers should be linked with the Employment Service and other labor market institutions and be governed by boards that include senior state government officials, business associations, unions, and officials from the local workforce investment boards established under the new job training legislation. These workforce development centers should be linked with the manufacturing extension centers that the Commerce Department currently supports, some of which have added labor specialists to help firms and unions on worker training. An alternative strategy would be establish these functions under the one-stop career centers called for in the job training reform legislation.

The centers would:

▲ provide research and information on education and training practices, especially "best practices" to interested businesses and labor unions;

▲ offer in-depth technical assistance and evaluation services to employers, business associations, and unions on a fee-for-service basis;

▲ facilitate and lead the formation of consortia of trade organizations, unions, and businesses to develop and provide training programs through start-up grants and loans;

▲ help companies understand the need to integrate training, work restructuring, and technology;

▲ provide support for service providers to develop training programs and pilot initiatives;

▲ offer incentives for collaboration and partnerships among institutions that provide training services.

These strategies will be especially important in promoting employee development in small- and medium-sized businesses. In addition, unions and business associations can play a critical role as training providers and as intermediaries between government and firms.

◆ *The federal government and the states should utilize workforce development centers to provide companies with information about training practices that have succeeded at other firms.* Only a small percentage of firms currently have workplace education and training programs that last more than a few weeks at a time. Many companies would like to develop more ambitious training efforts but do not know how to proceed.[54] Workforce development centers could disseminate information to local executives about how a variety of companies invest in the skills of their workers. Those materials would focus on:

▲ *Developing the skills of all employees and involving them
   in the process.* New workplace cultures can best be created
   by engaging employees in designing strategies for developing the skills and potential of every worker. Experience
   with "high-performance work organizations" supports this
   conclusion. These organizations emphasize increased
   employee involvement, group pay schemes, increased
   responsibilities for each worker, and training and education.

▲ *Increasing investments in worker education and training.*
   Only a small fraction of firms spend adequate amounts on
   the education and training of their workforce. The firms
   that do spend 3 or 4 percent of payroll on training tend to
   be larger, growing firms that are internationally competitive. Most firms should have as their objective increasing
   per capita training investments for incumbent workers
   through company-financed in-house training or partnerships with educational institutions.

   For decades, a majority of large firms have supported
   their workers' education as a routine benefit. Many of them
   have joint labor-management committees to administer and
   oversee training programs. Expanding tuition reimburse-
   ment policies should be a major priority of private businesses and their associations. Government can help by
   continuing to treat tuition assistance as a nontaxable benefit for workers.

◆ *Awards for excellence in human resource policies should be
   bestowed upon companies that demonstrate unusual efforts at
   enhancing the skills of their workers.* Representatives from
   government, companies, unions, and academia should emulate
   the successful precedent of the Malcolm Baldrige Quality
   Awards in the United States and the "Investors in People" program in the United Kingdom. The Baldrige awards program
   has fostered continuous quality improvement strategies in hundreds of firms that participate in the annual competitions and
   thousands of other firms that follow quality improvement
   principles but do not enter the awards competition. The

Investors in People program, which is strongly supported by company managers and union officials, has stimulated more effective private sector human resource practices. Firms could use such awards to attract workers who are eager to join companies that emphasize education and training.

3. Encouraging Individuals to Invest in Their Own Skills

Workers, whether employed or unemployed, have the greatest stake in maximizing their human capital. Improving their skills will enable them to command higher compensation while increasing their job security. Even if firms invest more in workplace training, many Americans will still need to invest in themselves. Just as the Task Force recommends additional incentives for private firms, individuals should receive encouragement in the form of tax deductions, loans, and more flexible and useful unemployment insurance.

Recommendations

◆ *The federal government should provide tax deductions to individuals who pay for their own education and training.* Federal and state governments offer substantial support for young people attending colleges and universities on a full-time basis. The combination of grants, loans, and direct subsidies has helped to build the finest and most widely accessible higher education system in the world. But the long-standing focus on educating the young is based on two assumptions that have become less valid as the economy has changed:

  ▲ the skills that will last a lifetime can be acquired during primary, secondary, and post-secondary schooling;

  ▲ only managers and technical workers, whose jobs require college degrees, need post-secondary education.

The Task Force believes that incentives need to be established to help all individuals obtain the education they will need throughout their working careers, whether or not they have attended college. Just as policymakers concluded more than thirty years ago that public investment in higher education was necessary for entry-level workers, the Task Force believes that the national interest would be best served by creating mechanisms to encourage and help workers learn throughout their lives.

The Task Force recommends that the federal government establish a tax deduction to help individuals finance the costs of upgrading their skills. The write-off should be based on the principle of ability to pay, with those making the least income eligible for a more generous deduction than those who earn more. Qualifying expenditures could finance courses offered by a wide range of post-secondary institutions. Tax deductions would encourage people to invest in education and training, regardless of whether they are employed, and even if their employer does not provide benefits for this purpose. In early 1995, President Clinton offered a similar proposal, which would have provided tax savings of $1,500 to $2,600 for middle-income families and cost the government $7.5 billion per year when fully implemented. The Task Force believes that the investment would yield dividends for workers and throughout the economy. Because tax deductions do not help those who do not itemize or who do not pay taxes due to low incomes, programs targeted toward low-income workers like the Earned Income Tax Credit (EITC) should be sustained.

◆ *The federal government should expand eligibility for student financial assistance programs under Title IV of the Higher Education Act to assist individuals who enroll in training programs and courses on a less than half-time basis.* This reform would enable individuals to qualify for up to $1,500 in Pell grants and/or borrow up to $2,500 under the federal Family Education and Direct Loan Programs to finance their training and education. Loans should be provided only to individuals enrolled in courses of study that will improve their basic educational abilities or upgrade occupational skills.

◆ *The federal-state unemployment insurance system should be reformed to enable those who have lost their jobs to upgrade their skills.* Despite funding increases in recent years, programs that provide job search assistance and training for the long-term unemployed reach only a small percentage of workers who are unlikely to return to work with their previous employer. Job training reform legislation under consideration by Congress could further reduce the funds available for unemployed adults. It is therefore appropriate to consider the role that unemployment insurance can play in helping these Americans make the transition from one job to the next.

Unemployment insurance helps millions who experience temporary spells of unemployment, but it is not sufficient for those who remain unemployed for longer than the six-month cutoff period—one in five workers during the last recession. The Task Force recommends several strategies for connecting unemployment insurance recipients to job search and training programs without undermining the vital security that the system provides:

▲ Unemployment insurance recipients most likely to experience long jobless spells should receive early, intensive job search assistance and training. The states are currently implementing so-called worker profiling strategies as required by Congress in 1993. The Task Force believes that profiling must be carefully designed to identify vulnerable workers, not just to limit participation. Those who are most likely to be out of work for long periods are identified by examining their education level, job experience, and conditions in the industry, occupation, or labor market in which they work. But Congress did not provide adequate resources to finance the job search assistance or retraining for those the system identified as at greatest risk.

The job training reform legislation now under consideration in Congress appropriately encourages states to locate offices where individuals apply for unemployment compensation in the same place as the state employment service or other publicly funded labor information centers. But while some of the cost of job search assistance and retraining may be covered by programs funded under the new one-stop career centers, additional strategies will be needed to help workers who are identified as "at-risk" for long-term unemployment.

▲ *All* unemployment insurance recipients, under certain conditions, should be allowed to participate in training without losing their benefits. Unemployment insurance eligibility rules typically prohibit individuals from enrolling in retraining programs because they are required to make themselves available for any job openings immediately and to actively seek employment. They must seek permission to enroll in training in order to continue receiving assistance, but in practice that may be difficult. Few employment offices regularly counsel beneficiaries to pursue that option.

The Task Force recommends that government job counselors be equipped to assess which unemployment insurance beneficiaries are most likely to exhaust their benefits before getting a new job and advise those participants to enroll in qualified education and training programs. The threat of losing unemployment benefits upon enrolling in such a program should be dropped. This reform may convince individuals to invest their own funds in retraining—particularly if there is a tax break for those outlays—before exhausting their benefits. The change would be unlikely to have a substantial impact on the costs of unemployment insurance because people eligible for benefits during training would likely remain unemployed and consume the maximum benefits anyway.

▲ Individuals eligible for unemployment insurance who do not have sufficient cash on hand to pay tuition or training bills, and who are not eligible for student loans, should be permitted to collect up to 30 percent of the unemployment compensation benefits to which they are entitled in a lump sum to help finance the cost of qualified occupational training. This change would require minimal additional resources while providing advance payment of funds that individuals would probably receive anyway. This change would enable the many unemployed Americans whose personal budgets are too tight to pay for schooling to make the sizable up-front payments required for many educational programs.

▲ The federal unemployment surcharge of 0.2 percent that is scheduled to expire in 1999 should be retained for investment in the skills of American workers. The Task Force recommends that the surcharge be earmarked for strengthening the nation's labor market information network and/or assisting Americans whose unemployment extends beyond six months.

▲ Federal and state resources for the workplace learning programs that the Task Force advocates also should be extended to unemployment insurance recipients who are at greatest risk of long-term unemployment. Companies, business and trade associations, or consortia of firms and labor unions would receive subsidies to train unemployed workers whom they intend to hire. Individuals would be permitted to continue to receive unemployment insurance payments during that formal classroom training.

♦ *In partnership with business and labor organizations, the federal government should mount an energetic campaign to educate workers about the need for lifelong learning.* Numerous researchers have demonstrated the high return to individuals on investment in education, yet many adults are unaware of the value of further education beyond high school or even a four-year college.[55]

Previous federal educational efforts to improve adult literacy, reduce drug usage, and halt the spread of AIDS have proven the value of well-orchestrated, well-funded, public information campaigns. A new "Learn to Earn" initiative should be directed at adults in the workforce and include information on the value of lifelong learning and how they can upgrade their skills. This campaign should be a joint public-private initiative with contributions from education and training institutions, private firms, and the government.

4. HELPING WORKERS WHEN FIRMS DOWNSIZE

The Task Force urges private firms to rethink their downsizing strategies in light of the mounting evidence about potential negative consequences, not only for workers, but for companies themselves. There is ample evidence that merely shedding employees without regard to their needs or the impact of downsizing on the survivors is counterproductive.[56] Initially, management gurus claimed that downsizing was a "risk-free" endeavor,[57] and many firms still contend they can slash workforces with few negative consequences. But downsizing strategies often ignore the workforce skills, company loyalty, and employee stability that firms need to remain competitive over the long term. Downsizing is a "quick fix" to corporate woes that can cause damage that lasts for years.

While some firms save money and achieve greater productivity by cutting their workforce, others experience losses in productivity, quality, and other negative by-products, such as a disgruntled or demoralized workforce. The long-term impact of downsizing for companies often hinges on how the layoffs are handled. Empirical research on corporate downsizing strongly suggests that many firms are doing a poor job of implementing cutbacks. For example, only one-third of the firms responding to American Management Association Surveys from 1989 to 1994 reported increases in productivity following downsizing; only half reported increases in profits.[58]

Companies that have fared well after downsizing often undertook efforts to help those who were laid off while investing in the workers who remained behind. Because the success of many firms hinges on factors such as the quality of service that employees provide to customers, workers who are discouraged and insecure about their future can undermine profits.[59] Yet, the most common approach to downsizing is an "across-the-board, grenade-type approach" according to a study of over 150 firms.[60] Eighty-six percent of the firms that participated in the 1994 American Manufacturing Association study of downsizing reported declines in employee morale.[61] The workers who survive lose confidence in the firm, experience high stress levels, and question their futures with the company.[62] These workers often seek more secure employment opportunities elsewhere. "Since there is so much employee distrust . . . workers aren't enthused about their jobs and putting in the effort they once did. There is a big turnoff at every level of corporate life," according to William J. Morin, CEO of Drake Beam Morin, a leading outplacement firm.[63]

Better treatment of displaced workers will help them and the nation's economy, but it will also sustain the morale and loyalty of those who remain at the firm. Research on corporate downsizing concludes that several practices help laid-off workers find better jobs more quickly, while helping firms to manage their remaining workforce.[64] For example, many firms believe that advance notice to employees will hurt productivity. But research by the Conference Board has shown that advance notice actually improves productivity when combined with other programs of assistance. [65]

RECOMMENDATION

+ *The Task Force recommends that private firms follow guidelines that have been endorsed by the Business Roundtable and the Committee for Economic Development, when undertaking workforce reductions.*

  Those guidelines are:

  ▲ Firms should think first about redeploying and retraining workers before laying them off.

  ▲ When downsizing, firms should communicate openly with affected employees and provide them with greater advance notice than is commonplace.

  ▲ Laid-off workers and their unions should also be involved in the design and implementation of worker adjustment strategies.

  ▲ Job search assistance should be provided to help workers who often have little knowledge of how to look for work in today's labor market.

  ▲ The firm's assistance program should be coordinated with government-sponsored job placement and retraining interventions.[66]

Not enough private companies follow all these strategies, unless they are forced to abide by union contracts. There are exceptions, however. Companies like General Electric, Duracell, and Stroh's have demonstrated that concern for laid-off individuals is consistent with concerns about the vitality of their firms.[67]

NOTES

1. Louis Uchitelle, "Moonlighting Plus: 3-Job Families Are on the Rise," *New York Times*, August 16, 1994, p. D18.

2. Tamar Lewin, "Low Pay and Closed Doors Greet Young in Job Market," *New York Times,* March 10, 1994, p. B12.

3. Kenneth Jost, "Downward Mobility," *CQ Researcher*, July 23, 1993, p. 627.

4. U.S. Council of Economic Advisers, *Economic Report of the President, 1994* (Washington, D.C.: U.S. Government Printing Office, 1994), p. 316.

5. U.S. Department of Labor, *The Changing Labor Market and the Need for a Reemployment Response* (Washington, D.C.: U.S. Government Printing Office, December 1993), pp. 4–5.

6. Kim S. Cameron, "Successful Strategies for Organizational Downsizing," *Human Resource Management* 33, no. 2 (Summer 1994): 190.

7. Lewin, "Low Pay and Closed Doors Greet Young in Job Market," pp. A1, B12.

8. Virginia du Rivage, ed., *New Policies for the Part-Time and Contingent Workforce* (Armonk, N.Y.: M. E. Sharpe, 1992).

9. Chris Tilly, "Reasons for the Continuing Growth of Part-time Employment," *Monthly Labor Review* 118 (March 1991): 10–11.

10. Keith Bradsher, "Widest Gap in Incomes? Research Points to U.S.," *New York Times*, October 27, 1995, p. D2.

11. Lawrence Mishel, *The State of Working America—1994–95* (Washington, D.C.: Economic Policy Institute, 1994), pp. 165–67.

12. George J. Church, "We're #1 and It Hurts," *Time,* October 24, 1994, p. 55.

13. John Cassidy, "Who Killed the Middle Class?" *New Yorker,* October 16, 1995, p. 120. Both high school graduates and Americans without high school degrees who attend career schools earn substantially more than those who do not; career school graduates who receive associate degrees benefit significantly more than those who attend such schools for one year or less without receiving an associate degree.

14. See, for example, Charles Brown, "Empirical Evidence on Private Training," in *Research in Labor Economics,* R. Ehrenberg, ed., (Greenwich, Conn.: JAI Press, 1990); Lisa Lynch, "Private Sector Training and the Earnings of Young Workers," *American Economic Review* 82 (March 1992): 299.

15. Lee Lillard and Hong Tan, *Private Sector Training: Who Gets It and What Are Its Effects?* (Santa Monica, Calif.: Rand Corporation, March 1986).

16. Max Carey, U.S. Department of Labor, *How Workers Get Their Training* (Washington, D.C: U.S. Government Printing Office, 1985).

17. Organization for Economic Cooperation and Development, *Education at a Glance: OECD Indicators* (Paris: OECD, 1995), pp. 28–29.

18. Ibid., pp. 153–54.

19. National Science Foundation, *Investing in Human Resources: A Strategic Plan for the Human Capital Initiative* (Washington, D.C.: Government Printing Office, 1994), p. 4.

20. Anthony Carnevale and Johnston, *Training America* (Alexandria, Va.: American Society for Training and Development, 1989).

21. Duane Leigh, *Assisting Workers Displaced by Structural Change: An International Perspective* (Kalamazoo, Mich.: Upjohn Institute, 1995).

22. Commission of European Communities, *Growth, Competitiveness, Employment: The Challenges and Ways Forward into the 21st Century* (Brussels: European Commission, 1993), p. 17.

23. Organization for Economic Cooperation and Development, *The OECD Jobs Study: Implementing the Strategy* (Paris: OECD, 1995), p. 28.

24. Ibid., p. 28.

25. U.S. Department of Labor, *What's Working and What's Not: A Summary of Research on the Economic Impacts of Employment and Training Programs* (Washington, D.C.: U.S. Government Printing Office, 1995), p. 45.

26. Scott Liddell and Dayna Ashley-Oehm, *Adult Workers: Retraining the American Workforce* (Washington, D.C.: National Conference of State Legislatures, 1995), p. 6.

27. Carnevale and Johnston, *Training America*, pp. 5, 48.

28. See, for example, AFL-CIO, *Labor's Key Role in Workplace Training* (Washington, D.C., September 1994).

29. David Levine, *Reinventing the Workplace: How Business and Employees Can Both Win* (Washington, D.C.: The Brookings Institution, 1995); Mark Huselid, "The Impact of Human Resource Management Practices on Turnover, Productivity, and Coporate Financial Performance," *Academy of Management Journal* (July 1995).

30. The Conference Board, *Partnerships for a Prepared Work Force,* Report No. 1078–94–CII (New York: The Conference Board, 1994), p. 11.

31. Anthony P. Carnevale, "The Learning Enterprise," *Training and Development Journal* 43, no. 2 (February 1989): 29.

32. Carnevale and Johnston, *Training America*, p. 5.

33. *Ibid,*. pp. 55–56.

34. See, for example, National Association of Manufacturers, *The Smart Workplace: Developing High-Performance Work Systems* (Washington, D.C., November 1994), p. 10.

35. Rosabeth Moss Kanter, "Nice Work if You Can Get It: The Software Industry as a Model for Tomorrow's Jobs," *American Prospect,* Fall 1995, p. 58.

36. Rosemary Batt and Paul Osterman, *A National Policy for Workplace Training: Lessons from State and Local Experiments* (Washington, D.C.: Economic Policy Institute, 1993), p. 17.

37. National Association of Manufacturers, *The Smart Workplace,* p. 10.

38. Laurie K. Bassi, "Workplace Education for Hourly Workers," *Journal of Policy Analysis and Management* 13, no. 1, pp. 55–74.

39. Ann Bartel, "Productivity Gains from the Implementation of Employee Training Programs," *Industrial Relations* (forthcoming).

40. Adrienne Eaton and Paula Voos, "Unions and Contemporary Innovations in Work Organization, Compensation, and Employee Participation," in *Unions and Economic Competitiveness,* Lawrence Mishel and Paula Voos, eds. (Armonk, N.Y.: M.E. Sharpe, 1992); David Levine and Laura D'Andrea Tyson "Participation, Productivity and the Firm's Environment," in *Paying for Productivity,* Alan S. Blinder, ed. (Washington, D.C.: The Brookings Institution, 1990); William Cook, *Labor-Management Cooperation: New Partnerships or Going in Circles?* (Kalamazoo, Mich.: Upjohn Institute, 1990); Mary Ellen Kelley and Bennett Harrison, "Unions, Technology, and Labor-management Cooperation," in *Unions and Economic Competitiveness.*

41. U.S. Department of Commerce, Bureau of the Census, *Statistical Abstract of the United States, 1994* (Washington, D.C.: U.S. Government Printing Office, 1994), p. 151.

42. Information about state-funded programs is derived from a survey of administrators conducted from March through May of 1994 by the Eagleton Institute of Politics, Rutgers University. Although other studies have reported that up forty-four states operate training programs, programs that are not targeted at the long-term unemployed or dislocated worker have been excluded. See, for example, Peter A. Creticos, Steve Duscha, and Robert G. Sheets, "State Financed, Customized Training Programs: A Comprehensive Survey," A Report Submitted to the Office of Technology Assessment, U.S. Congress, DeKalb, Illinois, September 20, 1990.

43. California Employment and Training Panel, *Annual Report 1992–93* (Sacramento, Calif., 1993), pp. 5, 20. These findings may exaggerate the positive benefits because there was no control group.

44. Philip Richardson, et al., *Referral of Long-Term Unemployment*

Insurance Claimants to Reemployment Services, U.S. Department of Labor Occasional Paper 89–2, Washington, D.C., 1989.

45. U.S. Department of Labor, *What's Working and What's Not,* p. 48.

46. Ibid., p. 53.

47. National Alliance of Business, *Approaches to Forming a Learning Consortium,* Washington, D.C., December 1995.

48. A Price Waterhouse survey found that "28% of the companies believe they could borrow for workforce training, [while] nearly 60% of employers believe that they would be unlikely to obtain such a loan." (Price Waterhouse, *U.S. Business Views on Workforce Training,* April 15, 1994.)

49. Peter A. Creticos and Robert G. Sheets, *Evaluating State-Financed Workplace-Based Retraining Programs: A Report on the Feasibility of a Business Screening and Performance Outcome Evaluation System* (Washington, D.C.: National Commission for Employment Policy, May 1990); Batt and Osterman, *A National Policy for Workplace Training.*

50. See for example, Electronics Industries Foundation, *Raising the Skills Standard: Electronics Technicians Skills for Today and Tomorrow* (Washington, D.C., June 1994); National Retail Federation, *Raising Retail Standards* (Washington, D.C., October 1994).

51. Carl E. Van Horn, *Enhancing the Connection between Higher Education and the Workplace* (Denver, Colo.: Education Commission of the States/State Higher Education Executive Officers, 1995).

52. Community colleges and private career colleges enroll nearly 85 percent of the full-time students who receive post-secondary education in specific vocations. (JBL Associates, *A Profile of the National Labor Market and Implications for American Education* [Washington, D.C.: The Career Training Foundation, January 1992], p. 14.)

53. For a similar proposal, see Laurie J. Bassi, *Getting to Work* (Unpublished manuscript, Public Policy Program, Georgetown University, Washington, D.C., 1995).

54. Laurie J. Bassi, *Smart Workers, Smart Work: A Survey of Small Businesses on Workplace Education And Reorganization of Work* (Washington, D.C.: Southport Institute for Policy Analysis, 1992).

55. See, for example, W. Norton Grubb, *The Returns to Education and Training in the Sub-Baccalaureate Labor Market: Evidence from the Survey of Income and Program Participation, 1984–1990* (National Center for Research in Vocational Education, University of California-Berkeley, May 1995); W. Norton Grubb, "Economic Benefits of Sub-Baccalaureate Education," (Report prepared for the Association for the Study of Higher Education Conference, Orlando, Fla., November 1995);

T. Kane and C. Rouse, "Labor Market Returns to Two and Four-year Colleges," *American Economic Review* 85, no. 3 (Winter 1995): 600–614.

56. See, for example, Chapter 2 of the background paper in this volume.

57. Michael Hammer and James Champy, *Reengineering the Corporation: A Manifesto for Business Revolution* (New York: Harper Business, 1993).

58. American Management Association, *AMA Survey on Downsizing and Assistance to Displaced Workers,* New York, various years.

59. James Emshoff, "How to Increase Employee Loyalty While You Downsize," *Business Horizons* 37, no. 2 (March/April 1994): 49–57.

60. Cameron, "Strategies for Successful Organizational Downsizing," p. 206.

61. American Management Association, *AMA Survey on Downsizing and Assistance to Displaced Workers,* 1994.

62. Richard Pinola, "Building a Winning Team After a Downsizing," *Compensation and Benefits Management* 10, no. 1 (Winter 1994): 54–59.

63. Daniel J. McConville, "The Upside of Downsizing," *Industry Week*, May 17, 1993.

64. The analysis that follows is adapted from Daniel C. Feldman and Carrie R. Leana, "Better Practices in Managing Layoffs," *Human Resources Management* 33, no. 2 (Summer 1994): 239–40.

65. Ronald E. Berenbeim, *Company Programs to Ease the Impact of Shutdowns* (New York: The Conference Board, 1986), p. 8.

66. See Committee for Economic Development, *Work and Change: Labor Market Adjustment Policies in a Competitive World* (New York: Committee for Economic Development, 1987), p. 34–36.

67. Case studies of several firms are offered in Feldman and Leana, "Better Practices in Managing Layoffs," pp. 239–60.

DISSENT

BY PHYLLIS EISEN

It was a pleasure to serve with the prestigious group gathered by the Twentieth Century Fund to examine worker retraining. I believe the issues were fairly examined, and all views were openly sought and encouraged.

We* strongly agree that education and training are associated with significant productivity increases and that companies that make steady changes in their human resource systems, i.e., move to high performance workplaces, are more quality driven, productive, and ultimately more competitive. We have spent significant resources and displayed a serious commitment to help our companies make these changes. Nonetheless, we have major concerns in two key recommendations in the final report.

1. We cannot, at the present time, support tax credits for training. In light of a recent NAM Board resolution to support tax reform, we believe it is unwise to layer, on top of an already inefficient system, new tax formulations. Although we recognize the need of small- and medium-sized companies to obtain resources for training, we do not believe that tax subsidies are

---

*The author is senior policy director of the National Association of Manufacturers (NAM); "we" refers to NAM, not to the Task Force.

the answer. Large companies are already aggressively increasing the education and training of their employees out of strict necessity; smaller companies are being pressured by their larger customers to do the same. Many large companies offer training at cost or seek innovative ways to leverage new resources for their smaller suppliers. A highly competitive global market is ruthlessly driving increased and highly targeted training and retraining for both current and displaced workers. We continue to support public private partnerships to both encourage new skills and high performance work activities. We believe in the increased involvement of business associations to drive this process and link their members with new practices, sharing of resources, and success models through a broad range of business-driven activities.

2. At the present time, we cannot support the use of unemployment insurance funds for other purposes. We disagree with the recommendation that workers draw down a portion of their UI benefits for training and the recommendation that the .2 percent FUTA surcharge be used for labor market information. Although we recognize the serious need for labor market information reform, the UI system is not the pot to dip into at this time. An increasing number of dislocated workers need these funds for the purposes for which UI was designed: for maintaining unemployed workers' living standards. The NAM believes that this social contract with its workers should not be changed, but does encourage a continued examination of reform in the UI system in these challenging times, and would welcome inclusion in that process.

DISSENT

BY JANE MCDONALD-PINES AND JACK SHEINKMAN

We are heartened that the diverse voices on the Task Force have arrived at such a strong endorsement of lifelong education and training opportunities for America's working men and women. Overall, we are convinced that the report represents an important step toward identifying policy options that would strengthen workforce education and training. We are pleased that the report acknowledges the ongoing contributions that workers and their unions are making in assuring high quality training in virtually all sectors of the economy.

Important as training is however, we consider it essential that our nation also maintain an unimpaired system of income support for those unfortunate workers who lose their jobs. Unemployment insurance payments help individuals maintain their living standards during periods without work. This safety net must not be weakened by diverting some UI Trust funds for other uses, such as training or labor market information.

We fully concur that employees need to make a greater investment in training, but we are deeply concerned that a training tax credit will not achieve the results desired. If a tax credit *is* adopted, it must include effective controls to prevent claims for training that would have been provided even without the tax credit.

To ensure accountability for public funds, any public investment in employer-provided training needs to be accompanied by
high standards and performance outcomes. These outcomes should
include practices that have been shown to be associated with high
performance work organizations, such as labor-management cooperation, worker participation in shop-floor decision-making, career
development opportunities, and reward systems for increased learning. The involvement of unions in workplace transformation activities is another key factor that has been associated with improved
productivity, product quality, job satisfaction, and employment
security.

A fully integrated approach to local labor markets will require
that any new university-based workforce development centers be
closely linked with a revitalized Employment Service and other
public education and training institutions.

Economic Change and the American Worker

Background Paper
by
Carl E. Van Horn

ACKNOWLEDGMENTS

The author wishes to thank several people for assistance in the preparation of the background paper: Aaron Fichtner, Amy Lesch, Eric Nauman, and Cynthia Smith provided exceptionally able research assistance at various stages of the project. Several individuals offered helpful suggestions on the draft manuscript: Greg Anrig and Dave Smith at the Twentieth Century Fund and William Gormley, Donald Baumer, Ken Ryan, and William Tracy. Ray Raymond of the British Consulate in New York City helped arrange a conference at Wilton Park in England so that the Task Force could examine international issues. His office also supported my research in England, Germany, and Brussels. Rutgers University awarded me a leave of absence for several months in 1995. The New Jersey State Employment and Training Commission supported research into the impacts of employment and training programs. The Eagleton Institute of Politics and the Bloustein School at Rutgers provided staff support.

THE BREAKUP OF LIFE AS WE KNEW IT[1]

The United States' economy is undergoing a wrenching transition. During the 1980s—a decade of strong economic growth and job creation—over 20 million people lost their jobs permanently.[2] The percentage of jobless Americans who remained unemployed for more than six months nearly doubled from 1980 to 1992, when it grew to 20.6 percent.[3] The average jobless period rose from three months in 1980 to four and one-half months in 1992. Not only is it taking the unemployed longer to find new jobs, they also are likely to earn significantly less than before when they do find work. More than half of displaced workers either remain unemployed a year after being displaced or are employed in jobs paying less than 80 percent of their former wages.[4] Fulfilling the American dream of permanent, full-time jobs with health and pension benefits and predictable increases in income may be more difficult than at any time since the early 1950s.

The current economic recovery has not improved the situation of the American worker. Over 8 million jobs have been created since January 1992 and unemployment fell to 5.6 percent in December 1995—nearly the lowest rate in five years, and way down from 10.8 percent in 1982. Yet, the percentage of Americans holding full-time jobs with health and traditional pension benefits is declining.[5] According to the U.S. Labor Department, "80 percent of the growth in the business sector has come not because more people were working more hours, but because the same workers were producing more for every hour they worked."[6] Nobel prize-winning economist Robert Solow points out, "You can't expect to grow just with efficiency."[7]

More significantly, since the early 1970s, 80 percent of the nation's households have not increased their incomes, despite increases in dual-income families and even three-job households.[8] In the past decade, median household incomes, adjusted for inflation, fell 5 percent.[9] In the 1990s, average wages increased by 2.5 percent after inflation, yet median incomes continue to stagnate. In 1993, for example, the median household income declined by $312 and a million more people fell into poverty, which reached the highest level since 1983. The reason is that, while the average wages of those in the top one-third of the workforce are increasing sharply, those in the bottom half continue to decline.[10]

College-educated workers are the only group whose real wages have not fallen in the early 1990s, according to the Economic Policy Institute.[11] While men with only a high school education experienced a 14 percent cut in earnings, after adjusting for inflation, the earnings of women who attended or graduated from college increased by 16 percent from 1990 to 1994.[12]

Massive layoffs persisted during the economic recovery. Large corporations announced over 600,000 permanent job cuts in 1993—a single-year record. In 1995, announced staff reductions totaled 439,883.[13] (See Figure 1.1, which reports data from Challenger, Gray, and Christmas, Inc., a firm specializing in outplacement services for laid-off workers.)

More than a dozen large companies have announced plans to cut up to 35 percent of their workforce since 1992 (see Table 1.1). Some firms, like IBM and GM, cut workers to staunch huge financial loses. Facing disaster in the early 1980s, General Electric eliminated 170,000 employees and increased its revenues by 150 percent by 1993.[14] Profitable firms, such as Xerox and RJR Nabisco, cut their workforces deeply, hoping for productivity gains. In short, downsizing is not the child of recession.[15]

FIGURE 1.1
Announced Layoffs, 1990–1995

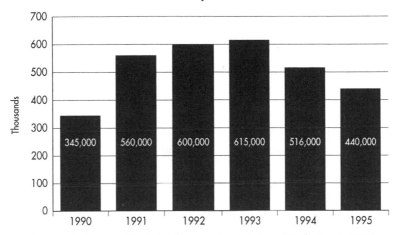

Sources: John Bryne, "The Pain of Downsizing," Business Week, May 9, 1994;
Challenger, Gray, and Christmas, as reported in Anne R. Casey, "USA Snapshots:
Downsizing 1995," USA Today, January 5, 1996, p. A1.

TABLE 1.1
Fifteen Companies that Have Announced the
Most Job Eliminations, 1992–1995

COMPANY	JOBS CUT	SHARE OF COMPANY WORKFORCE
AT&T	123,000	30%
IBM	122,000	35%
General Motors	99,400	29%
Boeing	61,000	37%
Sears Roebuck	50,000	15%
Digital Equipment	29,800	26%
Lockheed Martin	29,100	17%
BellSouth	21,200	23%
McDonnell Douglas	21,000	20%
Pacific Telesis	19,000	19%
Delta Airlines	18,800	26%
GTE	18,400	14%
Nynex	17,400	33%
Eastman Kodak	16,800	13%
Baxter International	16,000	28%

Source: "On the Battlefields of Business, Millions of Casualties," New York Times, March
3, 1996, p. 26.

The Evolution of a Transitional Economy

Widespread layoffs and long-term unemployment are not unprecedented in American history. Princeton University economist William Baumol argues that "what is happening to manufacturing today is precisely what happened in agriculture earlier in this century."[16] Other analysts would dispute this claim, arguing that the current transformation is more widespread and difficult. But, the more important point is that long-term unemployment is a serious problem today, and it has gotten worse during a period of strong economic recovery. Millions of people are experiencing permanent job loss and pressing public officials for relief.

During the Great Depression of the 1930s, millions of Americans were thrown out of work by a crippled economy. When the economy rebounded, millions returned to work as new jobs were created. The same patterns held during the immediate post-World War II era. As the U.S. economy went through its "ups" and "downs," workers were laid off as firms adjusted to slack demand for goods and services. When demand returned, so did the workers. This approach to handling the workforce gave private firms the flexibility to reduce overhead during slow periods, yet retain productive capacity for boom periods.

While American workers have never enjoyed government laws protecting their jobs—unless collective bargaining agreements contain "no lay-off" clauses, workers can be separated from their jobs "at will" by their employers—most joblessness experienced by adult workers in the 1950s and 1960s was temporary, the result of fluctuations in the business cycle rather than corporate practices. It was not unusual for workers to spend their entire working lives at a single company during the 1950s and 1960s, and many American workers felt like members of an extended family. Although the economic family experienced tough times, firm and employee shared in the economic boom and traveled together on the highway to higher profits and wages.

The comfortable relationship between worker and firm began to crumble in the 1970s. The American economy then began an arduous realignment that brought dramatic change in labor market practices and the nature of work in America. It became more common for companies to acquire or discard employees. Many laid-off workers never return to their previous employer and even profitable firms pruned their workforces.

Another foundation of the American labor market eroded under the intense pressure of economic change. During the 1950s and 1960s, the skills young people gained by completing high school enabled them to succeed in the workplace. Jobs paying good wages and requiring minimal education were abundant. Companies taught new employees job-specific skills, but such training usually did not take long because many tasks were not difficult to master.

In the current economy, low-skilled, middle-income jobs are disappearing, due to the sharp decline in manufacturing jobs.[17] According to the Bureau of Labor Statistics, while the percentage of high-wage jobs has remained the same since 1979, the percentage of low-wage jobs (earning under $400 per week) has grown—at the expense of middle-income jobs (earning $600 to $999 per week). The percentage of full-time workers who earn less than poverty level has increased by 50 percent since 1980. This pattern of low-paid, low-skill jobs is pronounced for young workers without college degrees.[18]

THE ANXIOUS PUBLIC

Public anxiety about working conditions and the economy registers in numerous public opinion polls and in voting behavior. Bill Clinton's election to the presidency can be attributed in part to fear over the nation's economic future. The same concerns also hurt the Democrats at the polls in 1994 and helped produce Republican control of the House and Senate.

Despite rising employment levels in the last two years, Americans say that jobs are scarce or hard to get.[19] A poll conducted for *Time* magazine in late 1993 found that two out of every three Americans believed that job security was worse than it was two years ago at the depth of the recession.[20] In October 1994, three out of five Americans told *Time* magazine pollsters that they did not feel they were better off as a result of the improved economy.[21]

Reflecting the reality of the changing economy, Americans complain about the lack of "good" jobs—stable, above average-wage jobs with health and pension benefits. For several years,

Americans have been telling pollsters that the quality of jobs available to them has declined in the past few years.[22]

Americans also worry about the future. A January 1994 NBC News/Wall Street Journal poll reported that 85 percent of Americans believe that businesses will continue to downsize.[23] In February 1994, two-fifths of those polled by the *New York Times* reported that they expected to be laid off or forced to take a pay cut during the next two years. One-quarter said that over the previous two years they had personally experienced layoffs, pay cuts, or reductions in hours worked.[24] And, for the first time in several decades of polling, a majority of Americans now believe that their children's economic future may not be as bright as their own.[25]

DISPLACED WORKERS ON THE RISE

Workers who permanently lose their jobs are known in the economics literature as *displaced* or *dislocated workers*.[26] Unlike those who experience temporary interruptions in employment due to fluctuations in the demand, displaced workers are not likely to regain their jobs. Job displacement may be caused by corporate restructuring decisions or because workers no longer have the skills required by the firm.

A high percentage of layoffs in the 1990s are really job eliminations. In 1992 and 1993, approximately three-quarters of job losers were on permanent layoffs and did not expect to return to their jobs. These are the highest proportion of job losers who are not on temporary layoff recorded since 1967, when such data was first collected.[27]

While the number of displaced and long-term unemployed workers fluctuates somewhat with the business cycle, human resource policies have been increasingly divorced from such traditional notions. For example, between 1979 and 1986, a period with two recessions, 5.1 million people were displaced. In the mid-1980s, when growth was stronger, over 4 million people were displaced from their jobs. Between 1991 and 1993, 9 million people were permanently separated from their jobs. On average, *more than a million people have been displaced every year since 1979.*[28]

Job cutbacks are often dictated by corporate perceptions of the need to cut costs for competitive reasons or to increase company profitability. Productivity benchmarks from U.S. and international competitors may be more important in determining the appropriate size of the workforce than the demand for goods and services. When America was economically isolated and dominant, U.S. companies were less concerned with holding down operating costs. Corporate survival and prosperity in the current economy means "running lean," with fewer employees.[29]

FROM MANUFACTURING TO THE SERVICES

The effects of America's economic transition were masked by the economic boom of the 1980s. Bolstered by government deficit spending, the nation nearly achieved full employment. However, just beneath the good news economy, significant industries were losing money and market share—and shedding employees. First, the auto, steel, and textile industries suffered. Then, the "boom" industries—pharmaceutical, computer, and telecommunications—stumbled. They also scaled back their workforces as they experienced the pinch of global competition and technological change.

At the beginning of the 1990s, the public and most policy makers associated long-term unemployment and displaced workers with the "rust belt economy." Many assumed that the economic malaise was concentrated by region, industrial sector, and class. Economic dislocation was a concern for people in the Northeast and Midwest, for old-line, heavy manufacturing, such as autos and steel, and for blue-collar workers. The phrase used to describe layoffs—"plant closings"—reflected the judgment that such problems were limited in scope.

This misperception of the economy was left over from the 1970s, when heavy manufacturing concerns such as the steel and automotive industries laid off thousands of workers and closed production facilities. Between 1979 and 1992 the domestic steel industry compressed, losing 321,000 workers or over half its workforce. By 2005, another 25,000 steel workers will lose their jobs, according to Commerce Department projections.[30]

Manufacturing was just the first sector to feel the effects of economic change, but permanent layoffs and economic dislocations would soon come to other sectors of the economy as well. In the early 1980s, one half of all permanent job losses came from the manufacturing sector. By the early 1990s, manufacturing accounted for just one-third of all permanent job losses.[31] In 1993, for example, retail firms, such as Sears, Roebuck and Co., and health care companies laid off more workers than manufacturing companies.[32]

Nevertheless, for more than fifteen years, manufacturing industries were exceptionally troubled: over 4.1 millon American manufacturing sector employees permanently lost their jobs between 1979 and 1989. Employment in just three manufacturing sectors—auto, primary metals, and machinery manufacturing—fell a staggering 50 percent *in just ten years* as over 400,000 workers permanently lost their jobs.[33]

As manufacturing employment declined, the economy created many jobs in the production of technology and the delivery of services. For example, in 1970 manufacturing comprised over 27 percent of the U.S. economy while services comprised 49 percent. By 1992, the manufacturing sector had shrunk to 16.6 percent; services had grown to 61.4 percent.[34]

The trend in the manufacturing sector offers important clues to the problem faced by many workers in America today. While manufacturing production and productivity are increasing, the production of above-average-wage jobs is stagnant. In 1994, for example, 90 percent of the U.S. manufacturers expected to increase production, but 60 percent expected to *cut* jobs, according to the U.S. Department of Commerce.[35]

An important question for the American economy is whether the new growth sectors—health care, information technology, business services—will continue to be job multipliers or will follow manufacturing's path, rapidly replacing workers with new technology. Thus far, the rise in service jobs opened up millions of jobs, but they are not the low-skill jobs once found in the manufacturing sector. The wage gaps between the old manufacturing jobs and many new service jobs are minimal, but the skills required in the new service-sector jobs are not those possessed by the manufacturing employees that have lost their jobs in the past decade. This has jeopardized the economic future of millions of displaced workers who find that their skills are no longer relevant to the new economy.[36]

FROM BLUE COLLAR TO WHITE COLLAR

As the low-skill jobs disappeared, many individuals with obsolete skills and limited formal education entered a radically different labor market from the one they had encountered ten or twenty years ago. "It used to be that someone without a high school education could get a good factory job for high wages and benefits and be set for the rest of his or her life. Manual labor jobs are not expanding anymore," says Daniel Meckstroth of the Manufacturers' Alliance.[37] Even while the economy created millions of new jobs in the 1980s, laid-off blue-collar workers had difficulty getting white-collar, service-sector jobs.

The *overall* unemployment rate for blue-collar workers has been significantly higher than the rate for white-collar workers in the most recent recession and recovery—9.9 percent versus 3.2 percent.[38] However, the gap between white- and blue-collar displaced workers has narrowed significantly in the last ten years. Twice as many blue-collar workers as white-collar workers were displaced in the 1981–82 recession (see Figure 1.2). In the late

FIGURE 1.2
Workers Displaced: Blue Collar and White Collar
1981–1990

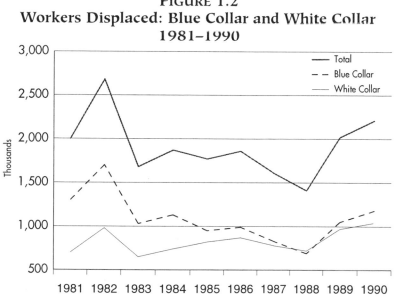

Source: Congressional Budget Office, Congress of the United States, *Displaced Workers: Trends in the 1980s and Implications for the Future,* February 1993.

1980s, there was no difference in the number of displaced blue- and white-collar workers. This is not surprising given the decline in displacement occurring in the manufacturing sector of the economy, as noted above.

Even the overall unemployment ratios are changing. The ratio of the *number* of unemployed white-collar workers to the number of unemployed blue-collar workers has been rising since 1982, the first year for which the Department of Labor has consistent occupational estimates. This phenomenon has occurred because the *ratio* of white-collar unemployment to blue-collar unemployment has increased, *and* because white-collar workers now make up a larger fraction of the work force than before.[39]

Middle-managers have been a prime target for many large-scale layoffs in the 1990s, as many companies have attempted to slash costs by reducing head counts.[40] The American Management Association's 1995 survey of 1003 companies that engaged in "downsizing" reported that 55 percent of jobs eliminated by firms between June 1994 and July 1995 were supervisory, management, professional, and technical.[41] In all, more than half of the jobs eliminated in the United States during this period belonged to salaried workers—who make up only 40 percent of the overall workforce.[42] In 1993, over 500,000 American managers with salaries over $40,000 lost their jobs, and between 1 and 2 million managerial positions were eliminated each year from 1991 to 1993.[43]

Financial institutions, high-technology industries, and service industries enjoyed the most success during the 1980s.[44] Many firms from these sectors expanded their workforces throughout the eighties, adding thousands of white-collar and skilled blue-collar jobs. But, other sectors cut workers because of the introduction of computers and robotics. Between 1979 and 1989, the wholesale and retail trade industries in America permanently eliminated 1.6 million employees; textile and apparel industries laid off 400,000 employees; 285,000 mining industry jobs were eliminated; and 479,000 transportation workers lost their jobs.[45]

America's dominance over production of consumer goods such as home electronics has also wasted away. Foreign companies, in the Pacific Rim and Central and South America, undercut domestic production by using cheaper labor and producing competitive products. The result: reduced demand for American-made products and sharp reductions in U.S.-based employment.

From a Wartime Economy to a Peacetime Economy

Huge increases in government defense spending during the 1980s also hid the nation's economic difficulties. After the Vietnam War, the U.S. significantly cut defense spending and defense-related employment dropped by over 1 million, from 5,839,000 in 1971 to 4,731,000 in 1976. However, by 1987, defense-related employment had jumped to nearly 7 million, with the majority of this surge occurring between 1981 and 1987. Most of the growth in defense-related jobs were in the private sector, not in the military or in government.[46]

When the cold war ended and military spending dwindled, thousands of high-tech defense workers lost their jobs. Between fiscal years 1987 and 1994, defense-related employment dropped by nearly 40 percent, with 25 percent of the losses occurring from mid-1990 through 1992.[47] Although defense-related jobs constituted only 5 percent of the U.S. workforce, the effect of 784,000 workers losing their jobs in less than two years created enormous problems for the economy. By the end of 1994, another 350,000 defense workers were expected to lose their jobs.[48]

The Problems Spread in the 1990s

When the 1980s boom ended, the underlying economic weaknesses became apparent. The severe recession of the early 1990s brought about increased unemployment and shifts in the labor market. Industries that had previously only known growth and prosperity, such as information technology and pharmaceutical firms, experienced financial losses and developed cost-saving strategies that included workforce reductions.

More than half of the United States' Fortune 500 companies have cut employees since 1989 and 100 percent are planning to downsize in the next five years.[49] All sectors of the economy, involving firms of varying size, are experiencing long-term unemployment and economic dislocation (see Figures 1.3 and 1.4, page 68).[50] In 1990, 60 percent of manufacturing firms were downsizing, but by 1995, this had dropped to 49 percent. Downsizing has now increased sharply in the financial and other services sectors. Heretofore unaffected industries, such as personal care products and food services, have also engaged in workforce reductions.

FIGURE 1.3
Percentage of Corporations that Have Downsized by Industrial Sector, July 1990 – June 1995

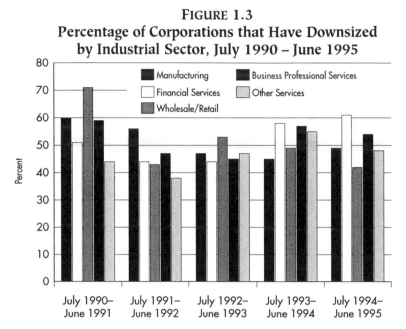

Source: American Management Association, *AMA Survey on Downsizing and Assistance to Dislocated Workers,* various years.

FIGURE 1.4
Percentage of Corporations that Have Downsized by Company Size, July 1990 – June 1995

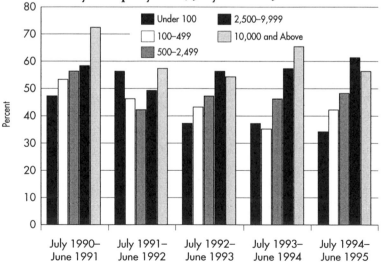

Source: American Management Association, *AMA Survey on Downsizing and Assistance to Dislocated Workers,* various years.

Large companies are more likely to cut their workforce than smaller ones, but the smaller companies eliminate higher percentages of their workforces when they downsize.[51]

THE RISE OF "CONTINGENT" WORKERS

As downsizing becomes a common corporate response to more competitive markets, "boardroom discussions now focus on what are called 'core competencies'—those operations at the heart of a business—and on how to shed the rest of the functions to subcontractors or nonstaff workers."[52] For example, IBM, once the icon of American job security, has traded 10 percent of its permanent staff for part-time and contract workers in the last few years.[53]

The American workforce is being divided into two distinct groups—an A team and a B team. The A team is the permanent group of "core workers"; the B team is the rapidly growing group known as "contingent workers." The temporary, part-time, and contract workers and consultants that make up the contingent workforce are employed to perform specific tasks for limited time periods. Contingent workers cut labor costs for employers because they are paid less and get no pensions, health benefits, paid sick days, and vacations. When their tasks are accomplished, contingent employees go to another job or the unemployment rolls. This fluid, less-expensive portion of the company's total workforce can rapidly expand or contract.[54]

The number of temporary jobs is increasing.[55] Part-time and contingent jobs have supplied much of the job growth since the 1970s. And most of the growth in part-time jobs consisted of involuntary part-time workers—people who would rather be working full time.[56] While voluntary part-time employment rose by 53 percent from 1970 to 1992, involuntary part-time employment increased 178 percent over the same period.[57] These trends are continuing during the economic recovery.[58]

There are no definitive numbers on the size of the contingent workforce, but the Bureau of Labor Statistics estimates that in 1995 contingent workers made up 5 percent of the work force.[59] In 1995, there were an estimated 6 million contingent workers. By 2000, the contingent work force could comprise one in three workers, according to one observer,[60] while another predicts that they will outnumber permanent full-time workers by then.[61]

The traditional notion of the temporary worker is that of the fill-in clerk or secretary who is dispatched to the office by a temporary employment firm. This view of the temporary worker is reinforced by the fact that two-thirds of all part-time workers and nearly 60 percent of temporary workers are women, according to the U.S. Department of Labor.[62]

The picture is more complicated today. For example, chemical firms are turning to temporary help at the professional level to handle research and development and other technical tasks. Temporary employment firms, which once supplied only clerks or secretaries, have reorganized themselves to provide high-skilled, technical workers.[63]

AT&T is an excellent illustration of a large corporation that is pairing downsizing with an increase in its contingent workforce. In January 1993, AT&T announced 33,525 job cuts.[64] Yet, approximately 6,000 new employees, many of whom will be contingent workers, were scheduled to be added in 1994. For example, American Transtech, an AT&T-owned telemarketing and temporary employment firm, announced a pilot project to place 200 of its temporary workers in AT&T jobs. They will earn $5 to $12 per hour and report to AT&T installations, but remain Transtech employees. Although the workers will have partial benefits, they will not approach the scale of compensation earned by AT&T's regular workforce.

There are many indications that the contingent workforce is on the rise. One of the nation's largest private employers is Manpower Inc.—a temporary help firm with 560,000 workers; during the 1980s, the temporary help industry grew ten times faster than overall employment;[65] more than 90 percent of the 365,000 jobs created by U.S. companies in February 1993 were part-time positions taken by people who would prefer to work full time.[66] Between 1990 and 1992, people forced to work part time because of poor economic conditions and lack of full-time jobs rose by 1.5 million.

Obviously, contingent workers provide employers with greater flexibility to adjust the size, composition, and cost of their workforces. There is nothing inherently wrong with part-time or temporary work. Many people, especially single heads of household with young children, prefer the flexibility that part-time work provides.

Frustration rises, however, when people who want to work full time are denied that opportunity. Moreover, the growth in part-time and temporary workers reinforces the gap between high- and low-wage earners. Bennett Harrison describes the process: "Work shifts away from the bigger, more established, sometimes unionized companies where workers are paid relatively high average wages and benefits, and where the gap between the highest and the lowest earners is relatively narrow."[67]

Analysts predict that short-term productivity gains due to lower labor costs will be offset by long-term productivity declines due to high worker turnover and low morale. The practice of hiring contingent workers can be used against "permanent" employees either to gain concessions at the bargaining table or to shift employment status. Many workers are involuntarily separated from full-time positions and then hired back as part-time workers to perform the same job.

The Engines of Change

There are many explanations for the economic transition under way in the U.S. economy and its effect on working Americans. Commentators usually cite the following: international competition and trade policy, technological change, an underskilled workforce, deregulation, stock-driven corporate planning, and interwoven networks or "alliances" of businesses. The combined pressures of these forces have encouraged firms to restructure their businesses and reduce their workforces.[68] Sorting out precise causal relationships is impossible because so many of these factors interact with one another. It is likely that economic change and dislocation has arisen for all of these reasons and more.

Competition

There is a widespread perception that greater competition among firms and between nations has transformed the U.S. economy and the nature of work. Whether this is in fact true or not, the need to shave labor costs in order to compete for market share is cited by three-quarters of the firms as a rationale for corporate restructuring and downsizing, according to a survey conducted by the Wyatt Company. In comparison, 37 percent said fluctuations in customer demand was the proximate cause of corporate restructuring. Even less important were technological advances, according to the survey.[69]

Economists Paul Krugman and Robert Lawrence are skeptical of the reported reasons for corporate downsizing and the emphasis on foreign competition as the cause of America's economic woes. In their view, international competition has little to do with the loss of manufacturing jobs in America or the decline of working American's incomes. Much more important, they argue, is the introduction of labor-saving technologies. Moreover, the reason that workers are being cut is because the new high-technology economy has less need for unskilled workers, not that jobs have been shipped overseas.[70]

Whether real or imagined, the fear of competition is shaping the behavior of many corporate leaders. American companies that manufacture at home and sell their products worldwide cannot compete in the global market on the basis of low-cost labor because labor costs are lower in Asia, Latin America, and Eastern Europe. Some firms may shift part of their operations to these low-cost countries, but U.S.-based firms know that they must concentrate on productivity, responsiveness, and quality if they want to compete with other industrialized nations and expand their share of the market.

The effects of the reality and perception of international competition is well illustrated by the American automobile industry. U.S. auto makers enjoyed a free rein in the marketplace in the 1950s and 1960s, but thousands of manufacturing jobs were lost when foreign automakers began producing cheaper, more economical, and more reliable cars.

The pressure on U.S.-based automakers was intensified in the late 1980s and early 1990s. To escape the "voluntary" import quotas, Japanese auto makers built plants in the United States; local and state governments have tendered generous tax breaks and subsidies in order to lure foreign automakers. Hondas are now manufactured in Ohio, Toyotas come from Kentucky and California, Nissans are made in Tennessee, and Mazdas are assembled in Michigan—once the sole domain of the "big three" U.S. automakers. The "state-side" strategy is also being followed by BMW and Mercedes-Benz, who are erecting new assembly lines in South Carolina and Alabama, respectively.

Foreign-owned plants that produce cars in the United States have caused U.S. job losses, according to several studies. An analysis conducted by the Economic Policy Institute estimates that Japanese-owned auto plants caused a net loss of over 150,000 jobs—primarily because Japanese automakers rely on suppliers in Japan for the parts needed to assemble their cars.[71]

The new plants are also of little help to laid-off auto workers because, with the exception of Mazda, they are located far away from closed-down U.S. auto plants. Japanese automakers also hire mostly young workers with little industrial experience and without union memberships. The transplanted Japanese production facilities also have lower health care costs and less costly pension schemes than their American counterparts.[72]

TRADE POLICY

Another hotly debated issue is the impact of international trade policies on economic performance and American workers. Whether specific trade agreements are net job creators or job destroyers, it is clear that new trading patterns often determine which sectors of the economy prosper and which suffer. International agreements, such as the North American Free Trade Agreement (NAFTA) and the Global Agreement on Tariffs and Trade (GATT), affect the location of production facilities. Cheap labor in less developed countries may influence U.S. firms as well as companies in other developed nations to establish more manufacturing centers overseas. The immediate repercussions of such trade policies may eliminate jobs in several U.S. industries over the next decade, but estimates of actual effects vary widely.[73]

Supporters of NAFTA and GATT argue that these agreements will break down trade barriers and improve access to foreign markets. If they work as expected, these agreements could create increased job opportunities for American workers. The President's Council of Economic Advisers estimates that NAFTA will augment export employment in the United States. They further assert that NAFTA will *also* boost U.S. jobs among union workers, frequently described as net losers, because of the new economic opportunities the agreement creates.[74]

Whether the ultimate impact of new trade agreements is an increase or decrease in the number of jobs, new trading relationships will dislocate workers in specific industries and regions of the country. As new markets open, firms that previously faced little or no international competition will be competing harder to hold onto their current customers. Inevitably, some firms will lose market share and job losses will result, while other businesses will flourish and new jobs will be generated.

TECHNOLOGICAL CHANGE

Early in the twentieth century, tractors and combines drove millions of farm workers off the land and into urban centers where manufacturing jobs awaited them. The current economic transition has no parallel outlet for the millions of displaced workers. Even though millions of jobs have been created in the last several years, many of these jobs require higher-skilled workers and those with college and professional educations. In 1994, for example, 72 percent of the 2.5 million new jobs were for managers, professionals, accountants, and high school teachers.[75]

Another reason for the differences today is that technological changes are happening more rapidly and affecting more sectors of the economy than before. In firms previously staffed with low-skilled or semiskilled workers, productivity-enhancing technologies, such as computers and robotics, now allow one person to perform the work of many.

Advances in technology have made it possible, and even desirable from the firm's perspective, to substitute machines for people. Fewer employees are needed to achieve stable output levels or even increased production. "Manufacturing employment is primarily governed by technology and new technology requires half the number of people in product assembly every six years," says Laurence C. Siefert, vice-president for manufacturing at AT&T.[76] Shoe manufacturers, for example, have been able to cut workers by adding computer technology to the design, manufacturing, and marketing of their products. Such changes are required to remain competitive with cheap labor producers in the Far East, but they have negative implications for workers previously employed in the shoe manufacturing industry.

Changes in technology have caused the elimination of entire divisions of companies. For example, in telecommunications, the once large, labor-intensive, long-distance phone units are now almost barren of human operators due to voice recognition and digital switching systems. The losses suffered by long-distance operators created new job opportunities for those who manufacture voice recognition equipment and computer chips, as well as those who repair and maintain the new equipment, but few of the displaced workers were able to make the transition from their former occupation to new ones in the telecommunications industry.

In the 1990s, demand will continue to plummet for electrical and electronic assemblers, industrial truck and tractor operators, typists and word processors, and textile machine operators. Demand will rise sharply for salespersons, nurses, general office clerks, waiters and waitresses, computer programmers, auto mechanics, medical assistants, and radiology technologists and technicians.[77] These "demand" occupations will create many high-skill, high-wage jobs for Americans, but without greater attention to retraining and continuing education, displaced workers will not be able to take advantage of these economic shifts.[78]

CONTROLLING WORKERS AND UNIONS

Critics maintain that corporate cost-cutting practices are motivated by a desire to gain greater control over their workers.[79] "Reducing incomes is exactly the point of this entire restructuring exercise," says economist A. Gary Shilling.[80] Deregulation of labor markets and threats of downsizing give many companies the upper hand in collective bargaining negotiations. Businesses insist that they need flexibility to respond to national and international competition, but unions are certain that such tactics are a ploy to soften wage and benefit demands.

BOOSTING STOCK PRICES

Critics also claim that corporations often undertake layoffs or plan larger ones than needed in order to boost short-term stock prices. This obviously pleases stockholders and investment fund managers. It also makes their firms more attractive targets for corporate takeovers and mergers.

The focus on short-term investment and speculation in market shares drives corporate decisionmaking toward actions aimed at quick returns—which often includes downsizing. In fact, announcements of cutbacks bring almost universal acclaim on Wall Street. The first day after announcing job cutbacks, IBM's stock rose 7.7 percent, McDonnell Douglas's jumped 7.9 percent, and Xerox's went up 7 percent.[81]

While some brokerage analysts applaud downsizing schemes, others remain very skeptical. Although the announcement of a labor-cutting decision may spike stock prices in the short run, Mitchel & Company, a consulting firm, reported that stock prices of firms that cut workers in the 1980s lagged behind the industry average at the beginning of the 1990s.[82] For example, American Express spun off Lehman Brothers in June 1994 in an ongoing effort to slash head counts. Employees and competitors criticized American Express for creating a "brain drain" and losing its employee talent—valuable to the company in the long run.[83]

Telecommunications companies have exploited Wall Street's enchantment with layoffs, announcing downsizing efforts to boost stock prices. Two U.S. West employees claimed that their company disclosed their downsizing efforts months before any planned action simply to drive up the value of company stock. The first day after announcing 9,000 layoffs, stock prices jumped 4.6 percent.[84]

The Communications Workers of America (CWA) president and U.S. West technician Mike Rea charged that, "the stock went up because Wall Street likes that they're going to reduce employees." U.S. West Spokesman Tom Johnson countered that the advance warning was to give employees ample notice to make plans for their futures, not for market reasons. However, many employees heard the announcement for the first time not from the company, but from a New York radio station. U.S. West claimed it had to announce the news publicly first to prevent insider trading of company stock.[85]

THE PAIN OF DISLOCATION

Unemployment has always brought misery to the unemployed—the loss of income, pride, dignity, self-esteem, and social networks. The unemployed experience higher rates of drug and alcohol abuse, spousal and child abuse, and separation and divorce than those who have stable jobs. The greater a displaced person perceives his or her economic loss, the higher their social isolation, the lower their individual vigor, the lower their self-esteem and the more stress they experience.

There has been a marked increase in the *length* of unemployment for those laid-off in the 1990s (see Figure 1.5). In 1970, 5.7 percent of the jobless were classified as long-term unemployed (without work for more than twenty-six weeks). In 1980, 10.7 percent of the jobless were long-term unemployed. By 1994, with an overall unemployment rate of 6.1 percent, the long-term unemployed constituted 17 percent of all jobless Americans.[86]

Workers displaced from their jobs clearly have difficulty finding comparable jobs. Since 1984, the Bureau of Labor Statistics has surveyed displaced workers to determine their labor force status. A Bureau of Labor Statistics study examined the experiences of those who lost full-time wage and salary jobs between 1987 and 1992. The results (summarized in Figure 1.6, page 78) show that only 27 percent of displaced workers found full-time jobs with

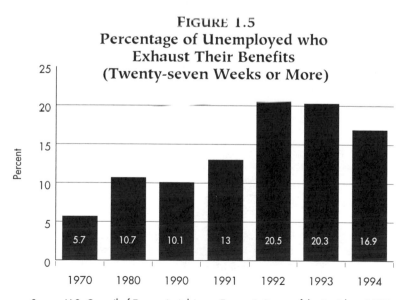

FIGURE 1.5
Percentage of Unemployed who
Exhaust Their Benefits
(Twenty-seven Weeks or More)

Source: U.S. Council of Economic Advisers, *Economic Report of the President, 1995* (Washington, D.C.: Government Printing Office, 1995), p. 322.

earnings equal to or higher than those on their previous job. Another 26 percent had found full-time jobs, but were earning less than before. Over one-third were unemployed or not in the labor force.[87] For example, of the several million managers who lost jobs between 1989 and 1993, over half took pay cuts of 30 to 50 percent to obtain new jobs.[88]

While large-scale worker displacement was originally a factor in declining industries and occupations, the incidences of displacement have become more widely distributed than ten years ago. In other words, the service-producing industries now make up a greater proportion of overall job displacement than they did a decade ago.[89] Workers laid off from the service sector fared better than those cut from the goods-producing industries. People laid off from manufacturing, construction, transportation, and public utilities were more likely to have substantially lower earnings in their new jobs.[90]

Another comprehensive study, funded by the Upjohn Institute, examined the phenomenon of worker displacement from 1980 to 1986.[91] Researchers compared postdisplacement wages with wages that individuals would have received from their former employers had they not been laid-off. Workers experienced losses of $9,000 or 40 percent compared with predisplacement earnings. After five years,

FIGURE 1.6
Worker Employment and Earnings after Displacement

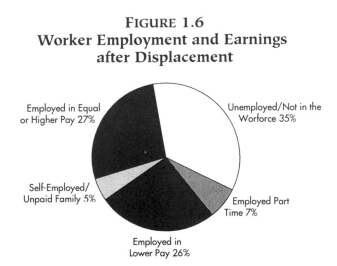

Employed in Equal or Higher Pay 27%

Unemployed/Not in the Worforce 35%

Self-Employed/ Unpaid Family 5%

Employed Part Time 7%

Employed in Lower Pay 26%

Source: Monthly Labor Review, June 1993, p. 18.

the losses were still $6,500, or 25 percent of pre-displacement wages. "If, as seems likely, earnings losses remained at about $6,000 per year until retirement . . . the present value of losses rose to approximately $80,000."[92]

The typical displaced worker is white, male, and of prime working age. About 42 percent of permanent job losers between January 1987 and 1992 were 25 to 54 year-old white males. Compared with their proportions in the population, "displacement is more likely among men than women, among blacks and Hispanics than among non-Hispanic whites, and especially among manufacturing workers. Despite the popular myth . . . older male workers (those aged 55–64) are no more likely to be displaced than workers aged 25 to 54."[93]

Experienced prime-age workers incurred substantial long-term loses. Five to six years after losing their jobs, they earned 17 percent less than if they had not been displaced. Moreover, these workers will probably never catch up to the wages they earned before separation.

Displaced workers in mining, construction, primary metals, transportation, communications, and public utilities experienced the largest reductions in income, according to the study. These are the most unionized industries in the country. Earning losses were smaller for displaced workers when they obtained new jobs in the same sector as their old jobs. The earnings of those in nonmanufacturing industries decline less than those of their counterparts in manufacturing, but recover at a slower rate.[94]

In addition to losing income, many laid-off workers, even those who were reemployed, lost their health insurance benefits. For example, of those workers displaced between 1991 and 1993, 72 percent had group health insurance through their lost jobs, but in 1994 only 53 percent had private health insurance.[95]

Long-term unemployment is most severe for minorities and those with the least formal education. Black workers experience longer periods of unemployment following layoffs than white workers.[96] African-Americans were the only group to experience a net job loss during 1990 and 1991.[97]

Unemployment has traditionally been a poorly educated citizen's peril, and the displaced workers who incurred the greatest losses in income were those who were the least educated. In 1994, for example, Americans without a high school degree had an unemployment rate of 12.6 percent, whereas 7.2 percent of high school graduates were unemployed and 2.9 percent of college graduates were jobless.[98] And while almost 90 percent of those with 16 or more years of formal education found new jobs, less than 60 percent of the displaced workers who had completed high school did so.[99]

People with a high degree of formal education are less likely to suffer the trials of unemployment during their lifetimes, and it should seem promising that Americans are better educated today than twenty years ago. Men and women are staying in school longer prior to entering the labor force. In 1970, 48 percent of the population 25 or older had not graduated from high school. By 1994, only 19 percent had less than a high school education. In 1970, 11 percent of adult population were college educated. By 1994, that figure had grown to 22 percent.[100]

Nevertheless, the most recent recession saw significantly more "educated" individuals unemployed than had occurred in previous economic slumps. This was especially true in the financial services and defense industries as highly educated workers joined the ranks of welders and mechanics on the unemployment line. While middle managers are only 5 to 8 percent of the domestic work force, they held 19 percent of jobs eliminated over the last five years.[101]

Large-scale layoffs can be particularly devastating in communities where one company dominates the local economy. The stories of such ill-fated towns as Flint, Michigan and Homestead, Pennsylvania are well known. The departure of corporate taxpayers and increased unemployment reduces local tax revenues while increased unemployment increases the need for social service expenditures. For example, in Dutchess County, New York, which was heavily reliant on IBM, there was a sharp increase in people treated in county mental health clinics after IBM closed its mainframe computer manufacturing plant, and the number of abused wives and other crime victims doubled.[102]

Communities affected by significant downsizing tend to follow one of several strategies, according to research on large plant closings.[103] Some adopt the "bystander" posture. Community leaders are passive as the firms go about the business of shutting down a facility and laying off its employees. Other communities try to "offset" the decisions of the firms by offering financial inducements such as tax breaks. Other local governments decide to become "players" in the decision to lay off. They pass laws making it harder for the company to leave, hunt for a new purchaser, or suggest new products that the company can produce.

In some instances, workers have successfully sued companies, forcing them to pay compensation to the town and the firm's workers. For example, American Home Products paid $24 million, approximately $10.5 million of which went to 800 laid-off workers. The company settled before a trial to determine whether the company had relocated a plant from Elkhart, Indiana to Puerto Rico to take unlawful advantage of tax breaks. In order to get tax reductions for new plants in Puerto Rico, the company had declared that no jobs were being displaced in the U.S.[104]

BREAKING THE COMPACT

In the post-war era, many employees thought they had an unwritten compact with their employers. Employees felt assured of lifetime employment as long as they worked hard for their companies. Employees would be laid off during hard times, and then called back as soon as the economy picked up. That unwritten compact has been broken.[105]

An employee at Pratt and Whitney captured the sentiments of many dislocated workers: "I feel top management has given up on employees. There is no sense of caring or concern over what happens to us; they're only interested in the bottom line. As a result, I'm a lot less concerned about what happens to the company."[106]

Speaking from the business perspective, Michael Hammer, a leading proponent of downsizing, says: "The idea that if I come to work, and I work hard, and I play by the rules, then I'll have a job forever—hooey. That's a naive fiction which we were able to indulge during an unprecedented and unreplicated period of economic growth."[107] Workers starting out in the 1990s are likely to have as many as six or seven careers over their lifetimes and therefore will need to retool their skills along the way.[108]

The meaning of work is changing along with the transformation of the economy. The new realities of economic dislocation undermine the faith in the motivations of business, the efficacy of government, and the "American Dream." (The expectations of mid-twentieth century workers are compared with what workers might expect today in Figure 1.7.)

Thirty years ago, most Americans assumed, with good reason, that their post-high school or post-college jobs would be permanent positions with good prospects for advancement. Health and pension benefits were part of the package. In the mid-1990s, expectations about one's working life are radically different. Says management consultant Barbara Collins, "People have got to look at employment as a temporary assignment."[109] Many Americans think they will never have a permanent job with increasing wages, health benefits, and a pension.

Instead of feeling a sense of belonging where they work, American workers are disaffected and fearful. "Whether you're downsized or outsourced, whether you're fired or continue to work, it'll be a completely different relationship—the idea of a large number of white-collar people working in one corporation, moving up and getting a pension is a phenomenon of the 1950s that is drawing to an end," predicts Dartmouth University professor Philip Anderson.[110]

FIGURE 1.7
Changing Visions of Work
in the Twentieth Century

Mid-Twentieth Century	Late-Twentieth Century
Permanent	Temporary/Contingent
Stable	Unstable
Advancement	Stagnation
Benefits	Some Benefits Provisions
Health Care	Some Health Care Provisions
Pension	Uncertainty About Pensions
Sense of Belonging	Disaffection

Views of unemployment are changing too. The old view was that job loss would be temporary and job searches would be short and successful. The new reality is that a majority of job losers never get their old jobs back and many new jobs pay less than previous jobs.[111]

Management analysts predict that we are witnessing the "end of the job." The influential writer Peter Drucker argues that the center of gravity in organizations has shifted away from jobs and toward knowledge. This, he argues, will cause enormous transformation in the lives of individuals and corporations.[112] Stable employment with an organization is being replaced by flexible work schedules, with people floating from one work situation to another. According to William Bridges, "the job is a social artifact, though it is so deeply embedded in our consciousness that most of us have forgotten its artificiality or the fact that most societies since the beginning of time have done just fine without jobs."[113] As more and more companies view jobs as "rigid solutions to elastic problems," more and more of them will be eliminated. He concludes that 100 percent of the workforce is temporary—no one has a permanent job—and urges companies to speak frankly with their employees about this new reality.[114]

SUMMARY AND ISSUES FOR TASK FORCE

The anxiety engendered by diminished expectations about economic security puts pressure on individuals, the American family, corporations, and governments. Concern for the impact of rapid economic change is echoed across the spectrum of opinion leaders. For example, U.S. Secretary of Labor Robert Reich argues that between the very rich and the chronically poor resides the "anxious class trapped in 'the frenzy of effort it takes to preserve their standings' as more and more families try to patch together two and sometimes more paychecks to meet their basic needs."[115]

The impact of rapid change is also widely written about by management gurus and in such mainstream business publications as *Business Week* and *The Wall Street Journal*. Writing in *Fortune*, business writer Stratford Sherman argues: "The era of revolutionary corporate change—still just beginning—promises enormous economic improvements at an exceptionally high cost in human pain." His conclusion: "As corporations abandon the unwritten contract of lifetime employment in return for hard work and loyalty, the social fabric of the U.S. seems weaker than at any point in the postwar years."[116] While this is surely a bit hyperbolic, it reflects business perceptions of the profound changes under way and their impact on workers.

Corporate downsizing strategies, their effectiveness, and the role played by unions are discussed in Chapter 2. The review in this chapter offers some insights into what corporations and unions might do to mitigate the counterproductive aspects of workforce reductions. Case studies of three economic sectors with extensive experience in handling economic dislocation—telecommunications, automobile, and defense—are examined in Chapter 3.

GOVERNMENT POLICIES AND THE NEED FOR REFORM

The analysis of private sector behavior, as well as contemporary government initiatives, points to the need for reforms in existing government policies to help people make the transition from one job to another. Policymakers have been slow to recognize the changing nature of unemployment and the need for more effective workforce adjustment strategies.

Federal and state policymakers have concentrated on improving *workforce preparation* in elementary and secondary schools for more than a decade. Just about every state in the country has reformed public school curricula and raised graduation standards. In the first two years of the Clinton administration, Congress passed laws establishing national goals for education reform and nationwide programs to smooth the transition from school to work.

Far less progress has been made in enhancing *workforce adjustment strategies* for displaced workers and for those already in the workplace; these strategies are discussed in Chapter 4.[117] Several state governments have undertaken innovative initiatives, and these are examined in Chapter 5.[118] Despite promising state experiments with pre-layoff interventions and company-based retraining programs, the federal government has not provided financial support for upgrading the skills of incumbent workers.

Federal tax policy mildly encourages retraining of a firms' existing workforce by allowing deductions for training expenses, but most of the training is spent on managers and executives.

The federal government's principal strategy for helping the unemployed is Unemployment Insurance (UI), an income-transfer scheme designed in the 1930s to cope with cyclical unemployment. In order to prop up demand and maintain people's standard of living, the government provides temporary and partial income replacement while a person seeks a new job or waits to return to his or her previous employer.

In fiscal year 1994, the federal government spent $31 billion on Unemployment Insurance—about the same amount spent on Aid to Families with Dependent Children (AFDC). Over $14 billion was consumed by laid-off workers who had exhausted the standard twenty-six weeks of benefits. While UI helps millions of Americans during periods of temporary unemployment, such strategies are inadequate when three-quarters of the layoffs are permanent and when millions of people lose jobs that they have had for a decade or more. Moreover, unconditional cash transfers do not help the society produce more competitive industries and highly skilled workforce.

For many, Unemployment Insurance is merely a way station on the road to long-term unemployment. After benefits are exhausted, typically in twenty-six weeks, many dislocated workers are still unemployed, looking for work. The current system does not require or even encourage people to invest in upgrading their skills or learning new ones.

A smaller federal program for dislocated workers, Title III of the Job Training Partnership Act, provides additional income maintenance and after-the-fact assistance in finding a job and getting retraining. Additional help is given to workers affected by government defense and trade policies, through the Trade Adjustment Assistance Act, for example. Determining which workers are "directly" touched by government policies is difficult, except for those in the defense sector. Policy choices about who deserves government support—timber workers in Oregon, textile workers in North Carolina, or computer chip makers in Massachusetts—reflect the political clout of various industries rather than a persuasive economic analysis.

In sum, contemporary workforce adjustment strategies are a hodgepodge of programs that do not meet the needs of large numbers of unemployed workers. Most federal programs do not even try to help people get jobs. Federal programs for the long-term unemployed are not coordinated and, not surprisingly, many workers and employers find them very confusing and inaccessible. Except for the innovative, but small experiments at the state level, government policy does little to support upgrading existing workers either to prevent layoffs or to enhance firm productivity.

The transformation of the U.S. economy has produced many tangible benefits, especially since 1992. Productivity is rising, unemployment is low, and inflation is in check. So what's the problem? Aren't the doomsayers about to be replaced by the optimists? Why should policy makers and private citizens be concerned?

Improving the public and private response to economic restructuring rests on four interrelated rationales: magnitude, fairness, economic self-interest, and politics.

MAGNITUDE. The whirlwind of change that is transforming the U.S. economy—new technology, international trade and competition, changing labor/management relations, new government policies— is leaving millions of victims in its wake. At any given time, there are over 2 million people in the United States who have been laid off permanently from their jobs. And those American who *are* working are doing so at a frenzied pace—with more overtime, longer work weeks, and two or even three jobs.

FAIRNESS. The effects of this economic conversion fall unevenly across the nation's workforce. Examination of any issue—increases in displaced workers, falling wages, involuntary part-time work, long-term unemployment—shows that minorities, mature workers, and those with the least education and training are experiencing the greatest pain. Millions of citizens who have worked hard and played by the rules are now getting hurt.

ECONOMIC SELF-INTEREST. The nation—individuals, companies, and the government—has not invested sufficiently in its workforce, according to most policy analysts as well as business and labor leaders. Underinvestment in education and training has detrimental impacts on the nation's standard of living.[119] The logic of the argument was stated by Harvard Business School professor Michael Porter: "Education and training are decisive in national competitive advantage . . . perhaps the single greatest long-term leverage point available to all levels of government." A better education and training system not only benefits the nation's economic productivity, but also specific firms. Porter's multination study concludes: "Those industries that were the most competitive were often those where specialized investment in education and training had been unusually great."[120]

POLITICS. Anxiety about economic progress undermines political stability. The customary economic indicators—low unemployment and low inflation—are cold comfort to people who are working harder and falling behind. When marquee companies—IBM, AT&T, Xerox, and GM—announce huge layoffs, people feel less secure about their jobs and their children's future. Rising risks in the job market have not been matched by rising compensation for most Americans.[121] As individuals in the middle class worry about their ability to hold on and become more frustrated about working harder to maintain their standard of living, the search for scapegoats is inevitable. Group bashing and blame shifting are widespread responses. The targets vary—the Japanese, immigrants, minorities, welfare recipients, and even incumbent politicians. The blame game will become more corrosive and dangerous, until people perceive that their government and the private sector not only care about their condition, but are doing something effective to help them.

WINNERS, LOSERS, AND SURVIVORS

The nation's economic transformation raises many questions for corporations and unions. What happens when firms decide to lay off people? How do corporations treat laid-off workers? Do companies achieve the results they want from layoffs? What effects do job cuts have on productivity? What role do unions play in downsizing?

A thorough investigation of private-sector human resource practice is important because unions, workers, and companies are still developing strategies for handling large-scale reductions. Sound public policies that aid companies and workers alike and government interventions to prevent and ameliorate layoffs will be more effective if policymakers have a deeper understanding of the private sector.

Unfortunately, corporate restructuring practices have not been sufficiently analyzed. Many corporations are not open to sharing information about their workforce strategies. Moreover, it is difficult to take a clear snapshot of the rapidly changing scene in thousands of businesses. There is also enormous diversity; companies take different approaches in different sectors, regions, and political and economic environments.

THE DOWNSIZING CALCULUS

The decision about whether or not to downsize is not a simple one. Private firms must balance organizational, financial, and political issues when conducting job cutbacks. Decisions about severance pay for laid-off workers are not just questions about the firm's available cash, but also how it wants to be perceived in the community and among remaining employees. Corporations are concerned about image, political backlash, and the potential for unionization or the impact on future collective bargaining agreements. Firms may also face legal actions from aggrieved individuals. Displaced executives collect more than $30 million each year in damage awards and settlements, not including payments made to individuals in suits charging age discrimination.[1]

LAYOFF ALTERNATIVES

Before laying people off and undergoing the costs associated with downsizing, many firms implement strategies to minimize or avoid layoffs. According to surveys of several hundred businesses conducted by the American Management Association from 1989 to 1995, only voluntary separations have increased over that period (see Figure 2.1). Hiring freezes, transfers, and job reclassification were also more popular strategies than early retirement schemes and salary freezes and reductions.

Worksharing, the strategy of cutting pay and work hours in order to avoid layoffs, is used commonly in Europe. Many European trade unions espouse shortened work weeks with corresponding reductions in compensation as alternatives to layoffs. For example, Volkswagen, a company owned in part by the German government and its workers, has, in the past, reduced its work week from thirty-five to twenty-nine hours and cut worker pay by 10 percent in return for guaranteeing jobs for the next two years. Governing parties in France and Germany are actively developing variations on this theme in order to guarantee a higher rate of employment. The advantages of a shorter work week is that it saves current jobs, but it also adds a powerful disincentive for creating new jobs.[2]

Such strategies are much less frequently used in the United States: 10 percent of the firms surveyed by the American Management

Association utilized job sharing and shorter work weeks or days as methods to avoid involuntary layoffs.[3] States and the federal government have attempted to encourage use of this strategy by making unemployment benefits available to those who work less than full time. Under these agreements, those working shorter hours receive regular pay for their work hours and a pro-rata share of their weekly unemployment insurance compensation for the days or hours not worked.

State-administered worksharing or Short-time Compensation (STC) programs were authorized in the United States under the Tax Equity and Fiscal Responsibility Act of 1982. As of 1993, seventeen states had such programs. Under these programs the work week must be reduced by at least 10 percent. If the state labor department approves the company's plan, the state will pay a percentage of the employee's unemployment benefits in an amount equal to the percentage of reduction in wages. In most states, firms are not required to maintain full fringe benefits, but most employers do so anyway. They are primarily used by firms to support workers at the beginning of economic downturns and as a supplement to layoff programs, not as a substitute for them. Unfortunately, there are no

FIGURE 2.1
Percentage of Firms Using Strategies to Avoid Layoffs, July 1990–1995

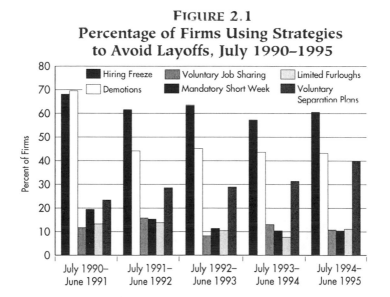

Source: American Management Association, AMA Survey on Downsizing and Assistance to Dislocated Workers, various years.

systematic evaluations to determine the extent to which these arrangements reduce overall unemployment in the economy.[4]

Despite the strong pressures for downsizing, many companies still maintain no-layoff policies. For example, Federal Express, Hallmark Cards, Honda, Johnson Wax, Fel-Prop, and Haworth, Inc. all have no-layoff strategies. When Johnson Wax, a world-wide producer of industrial and household products with 3,000 employees, encountered a decline in demand, the company retrained production workers as office personnel. Companies with no-layoff policies tend to invest larger than average resources in retraining employees and have a strong customer focus in their business practices. They also tend to rely on contingent workers and outsourcing to manage fluctuation in demand for their goods and services.[5]

A few companies have established productivity improvement plans as a layoff avoidance strategy. For example, Lincoln Electric Company in Ohio ties compensation to each worker's productivity and the profitability of the firm. Workers must meet demanding standards, but in return they are guaranteed no layoffs. The system has worked for more than sixty years, but it may have harmed the company because it prevented expansion during boom periods and the development of new product lines. Additionally, it has proved hard for many workers, who are denied paid sick days and holidays.[6]

Some companies use retraining or so-called inplacement or redeployment strategies to avoid laying people off. In this way, as one business unit declines, its workers are prepared to move into another unit that is growing. Or as a new technology is introduced, workers are retrained to use that technology rather than being forced out of the firm. Intel, the computer chip manufacturer, is a good case in point. The firm has five employee development centers. Employees are given the time and resources to improve their skills so that they can move into the company's redeployment pool and moved into new jobs as they become available.[7] States also fund retraining programs that are designed in part to avoid layoffs and long-term unemployment. (These programs will be examined in Chapter 5.)

Often, layoff prevention and no-layoff policies are achieved through collective bargaining agreements. Collective bargaining may produce union concessions in wages, benefits, and work rules, reducing costs. For example, the New York City Health and Hospitals Corporation and the unions representing 30,000 of its workers agreed in 1994 that workers would be protected from layoffs for four years in return for a one-year wage freeze and a reduction in the hospitals' contributions to employee benefit funds.[8]

GOVERNMENTAL CONSTRAINTS

Corporations face minimal government regulations on decisions about the size, location, and composition of their workforces. Laws governing private-sector labor market practices set out conditions for employee selection and treatment on the job, such as rules on health safety. Federal and state laws cover nondiscrimination, sexual harassment, and citizens with disabilities. There are few laws governing layoffs, and they primarily address issues of notice, discrimination, and harassment (see Chapters 4 and 5).

Nevertheless, firms consider government policies with respect to unemployment insurance, advance notice, and coordination of government services when making layoff decisions. Tax laws offer assistance to firms undergoing economic change and workforce reductions. Costs incurred in layoffs are tax deductible and therefore furnish a write-off against earnings. Companies charge billions of dollars against their earnings each year when they lay workers off. For example, NYNEX's reduction of 16,800 employees translated into a $1.6 billion charge to earnings in January 1994.[9]

Managers constructing separation packages for laid-off workers know that many people will be eligible for at least six months of unemployment insurance. The generosity of severance packages is often related to the unemployment insurance programs, as well as available cash. In these instances, companies require workers to apply for unemployment benefits and then deduct benefit awards from severance pay.[10] Employers must pay additional unemployment insurance taxes when they cut workers, but the increased taxes usually amount to no more than three weeks pay, on average, for each laid-off worker.[11]

CORPORATE LAYOFF STRATEGIES

Attempts to balance the needs of the firm with concerns about the reactions of remaining employees yield different layoff strategies. Some firms swiftly terminate and remove workers without warning—circumventing the weak federal statutes governing advance notice. Other firms furnish ample warning about impending workforce reductions. Some companies fund no severance payments and cut off health benefits immediately. Others dispense generous severance pay, extended health benefits, retraining, and relocation assistance.

Because most firms are not constrained by contractual obligations with workers or government laws, they can do what they want when they lay off people. Variations in practice are influenced by the underlying reason for the layoffs, perceptions of what is in the company's self-interest, and its experience with prior job cutbacks.

Another determining factor is the type of employee targeted for layoffs. Hourly workers do not receive the same treatment as salaried workers. Layoffs of supervisors, middle managers, professionals, and technicians are handled with greater sensitivity. White-collar workers in nonunionized firms receive more severance pay and outplacement services than their blue-collar colleagues.

The culture of the firm and its attitudes about its labor force play a large role in determining *how* job cutbacks are undertaken. Obviously, financially sound firms can afford to offer incentives for voluntary workforce reductions and larger severance packages. Healthy companies provide greater levels of support to displaced workers, but even among them there is tremendous variation in how workers are treated when firms restructure.[12] Given the impact that downsizing has on the morale of those who remain, many managers want to avoid the perception that layoffs are unwarranted or unfair.

Some firms are organized around narrow job descriptions, strict rules, and close supervision. In such firms, layoffs are managed from the top down with little advance notice and engender mistrust from workers. For example, IBM's hierarchical management culture did not facilitate worker involvement in its first-ever layoff in 1993. IBM was for decades the citadel of job security and strong corporate-employee bonds. Those bonds were shattered when IBM announced job cuts totalling over 50,000. In one day at the Mid-Hudson Valley facility, 2,700 employees were dismissed without prior warning. Workers were escorted from the building immediately and allowed to return only for their personal belongings.[13] Perhaps it is because IBM's behavior was so unexpected that this layoff event was recalled by more people than any other in a survey reported by the Roper Organization in 1992.[14]

Other corporations prefer greater worker discretion, flexible structures for employee performance,[15] and a corporate culture that supports open communication in addressing downsizing and how layoffs might be avoided. The corporate culture at Hewlett-Packard fostered a very different approach although its financial difficulties were not as severe as IBM's. Hewlett-Packard's management demanded cost-cutting measures, but committed itself to avoiding layoffs. Rather than lay off 10 percent of its workers, Hewlett-Packard reduced each employee's and manager's salary by 10 percent. The message of shared pain, conveyed throughout the corporation, helped preserve the loyalty of the firm's employees.

SHOW THEM THE DOOR

More than one in five of the 870 firms surveyed by the American Management Association (AMA) in 1993 extended no assistance to their displaced workers.[16] "Show them the door" downsizing strategies assumed that workers are liabilities as soon as the layoff notice is given. Fear of potentially dangerous, disgruntled workers prompts managers to remove workers from the place of business as soon as possible. For example, when Tenneco laid off 1,200 employees in Texas,

> many of them first found out they were no longer employed when armed guards appeared on their office floors early in the morning, along with boxes for them to use in cleaning out their desks. The stunned workers were given 20 minutes to leave the building, and were watched by the guards as they packed up their belongings and emptied their lockers at the company gym. Those managers who had come to work in company cars or van pools were given coupons for taxi rides home.[17]

Tenneco had the foresight to order hundreds of boxes for removal of personal items and have taxis waiting to escort displaced workers off the property. Yet, workers were given no forewarning of the massive layoff.

ADVANCE NOTICE

In 1988, less than four weeks' notice was provided to workers employed in 80 percent of the companies that laid people off. Many firms gave less than a few hours' notice.[18] Concern over the low incidence of advance warning culminated in the enactment of the Worker Adjustment and Retraining Notification Act (WARN) of 1988. This law requires companies with one hundred or more employees that are laying off fifty or more workers (or more than one-third of their work force, whichever is greater) to notify employees at least sixty days in advance. In lieu of notice, companies may offer sixty days of severance payments. Beyond informing workers of impending layoffs, companies are supposed to apprise state and local political jurisdictions. Several states have augmented WARN with their own legislation regarding advance notice (see Chapter 5).

Several studies conclude that WARN did not remedy the situation. The General Accounting Office estimates that the number of large firms giving advance notice has risen to only 30 percent in 1990.[19] Between 1991 and 1993, the U.S. Department of Labor estimates that 42 percent of *displaced workers*—those unemployed for six months or more—had received written advance notice.[20] The U.S. Department of Labor reported that less than 1 percent of the 331,000 people who participated in its job retraining programs in 1991 had received WARN notices.[21] The principal reason is that WARN exempts many layoffs. For example, if the layoff does not affect one-third of the workforce, then no notice is required. Many employers ignored the law's requirements or said they were unaware of them.[22]

Noncompliance with WARN is also a factor. Advance notice requirements conflict with many firms' desire to employ workers just as long as they are needed. Early notice is opposed because they fear it will decrease productivity, and that employees will seek employment elsewhere. Managers say that WARN is inflexible and insensitive to the reasons behind layoffs. Companies complain that compliance with the rule produces no information on benefits or retraining services for employees. Many companies say WARN compels them to immediately remove employees from the job site—

they would rather furnish severance pay than suffer the consequences of sabotage by disgruntled workers.

The apprehensions about advance notice are dubious ones. Announcements of layoffs and plant closings illicit an initial shock and drop in productivity. But, productivity may increase because employees want to convince managers to change their minds on closing the plant. Quit rates after notification are also low. In fact, advance notice is more likely an anathema to corporations because such information can have implications for the stock values of companies. Therefore, firms closely guard the timing of any announcements about restructuring and layoffs.

ASSISTANCE TO LAID-OFF WORKERS

Most firms offer transitional assistance to workers, including outplacement services, severance pay, extended benefits, and retraining programs to help with workers' reemployment. Three-quarters of firms provide outplacement services to at least some laid-off workers, according to the American Management Association's 1995 survey of 1,003 firms (see Figure 2.2). Outplacement assistance

FIGURE 2.2
Percentage of Firms Providing Aid to
Laid-off Workers, July 1990–June 1995

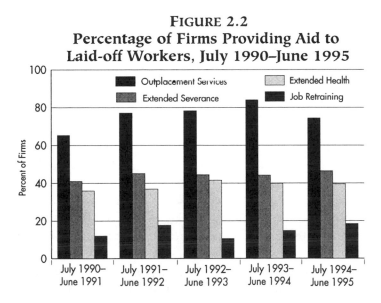

Source: American Management Association, *AMA Survey on Downsizing and Assistance to Dislocated Workers,* various years.

takes various forms—from full services by professional consulting firms to distributing lists of local employment agencies.

The AMA survey and other studies suggest that companies are becoming less generous with severance and job retraining benefits and relying more on outplacement services as the principal or only form of aid to their laid-off employees. "Employers are getting used to downsizing and they view severance packages as an on-going cost. Therefore, employers are inclined to be less generous than in the past," according to Janet Fuersich of Coopers & Lybrand.[23]

While most companies provide only outplacement assistance, a small percentage provide a full range of services to their laid-off workers. These companies spend time, energy, and resources to help those who have been let go. The Leaf Candy company in Chicago, for example, gave its workers two years advance notice, brought in instructors to help workers obtain their high school equivalency degrees, and set up an outplacement unit. According to plant managers, this compassionate approach to downsizing was also beneficial for the company because production, attendance, and safety problems did not worsen during the two-year period before layoffs occurred.[24]

OUTPLACEMENT SERVICES

Three quarters of all firms responding to the AMA survey furnished outplacement services to laid-off workers in 1995, but only 44 percent of the responding firms offered outplacement to *all* employees. As the least expensive form of assistance, outplacement services usually involve résumé preparation, the use of job directories and telephones, interviewing workshops, career counseling, direct placement assistance, and lifestyle and financial planning workshops. They typically provide assistance for a period of three months after termination. Some companies, such as Boeing, Wang, and AT&T, furnish office space, telephones, personal computers, and secretarial assistance for laid-off workers, while other companies work in conjunction with unions or government-sponsored programs. In these instances, placement centers offer a wider array of services and often function for one year or longer after the layoffs occur.

Outplacement programs yield positive benefits. Individuals who receive outplacement assistance are more able to enter retraining programs and even locate to another community in order to obtain employment. The laid-off employee can rely on a structured support system to cope with the loss. When Stroh's Brewery closed its Detroit plant, outplacement services for both salary and wage employees included skill testing and assessment, individual counseling and job search assistance, and computerized job banks. One year later, all of the salaried and 98 percent of hourly employees were employed in new jobs. When Ford eliminated 2,000 jobs at its Ontario facility, a worker-adjustment team—consisting of representatives from Ford, the United Auto Workers, and officials from the Canada Manpower Consultative Service—was able to place 85 percent of the dislocated workers.[25]

Not all outplacement services are of equal quality. During the first round of IBM's Hudson Valley layoff, the company failed to emphasize long-distance job search methods or supply an up-to-date national database of job opportunities in its outplacement program, even though approximately 40 percent of laid-off employees might have to relocate.[26]

Severance Pay and Extended Benefits

Surveys of U.S. firms indicate that between 40 and 65 percent offer severance to all employees, as opposed to just the top executives. Over four in ten firms responding to the 1995 AMA survey granted extended severance payments to workers who lose their jobs due to workforce reductions.[27] Examples of the types of benefit extensions offered include continued health insurance and continued life insurance.

Severance payments come in many forms and amounts. It may be paid in a lump sum upon separation or dispensed over several months. Many severance policies stipulate that former employees are entitled to payment only if they remain unemployed or find a lower paying job. If a job is obtained, the severance payment is often reduced.

The size and extent of severance and benefit packages are usually a function of years of service and level of responsibility, and are often expressed as a multiple of salary. For example, Digital Equipment Corporation pays workers with less than ten years' service nine weeks' pay plus a lump sum of one week's pay for each year of service. Those with ten or more years get the nine weeks' pay, plus a lump sum of ten weeks' pay and two weeks' pay for each year of service. The average cost per discharged employee is $40,000. But this is less expensive than Digital's first round of lay-offs, in which severance pay was higher and the average worker received $70,000 in payments and extended benefits.[28]

Severance payments are typically more generous in large firms and for white-collar employees and senior managers. Top executives do best with severance pay in part because corporations fear law suits.[29] Blue-collar workers with union contracts also fare better than nonunionized workers.

Another form of financial assistance is supplementary unemployment benefits. Corporations and unions can bridge the gap between government-funded unemployment insurance payments and the worker's average weekly earnings. Contracts in the automotive industry provide payments that guarantee at least 95 percent of previous income. Many corporations prefer this method of handling separation agreements with workers. By coupling the firm's responsibility with federal unemployment insurance, they reduce costs by 25 to 30 percent.[30]

Voluntary resignations and retirement are also induced through severance pay and extended benefit programs—a tactic used by four in ten firms.[31] Often, "voluntary" programs do not persuade enough people leave. Another problem is that high performers will leave because they have the best prospects of getting other jobs.

Severance pay and extended benefits allow displaced workers to weather the financial difficulties of unemployment by helping them maintain their standard of living while they enroll in further education or retraining programs. Health care is especially helpful to workers who are not eligible for Medicare. Financial assistance lessens the need for spouses to increase their workload and diminishes the urgency of accepting a job that pays substantially less than the former position.

JOB RETRAINING

Many individuals require job retraining to make the transition from one industry to another and from one occupation to the next. Laid-off workers who complete retraining programs spend less time unemployed than those who don't.[32] However, the evidence is mixed as to whether retraining programs have a substantial positive effect on future earnings (a point examined in more detail in Chapter 4).[33]

Though retraining may be valuable for many individuals, it is not surprising that retraining is rarely funded by private firms. Approximately 18 percent of these firms helped pay for the retraining of workers in the 1995 AMA survey as noted in Figure 2.2. "When you move away from the leaders, the large companies, or the ones with strong unions, there isn't a lot of retraining done, period," according to Ed Schroer, vice president of the American Society for Training and Development.[34]

Those firms that offer retraining obviously expect that they will recall laid-off employees. Under an agreement with its unions, AT&T is one of the few companies that offers retraining for laid-off workers. While the first priority is retraining employees for other jobs in the company, they will retrain people for work elsewhere, too.

Firms are very reluctant to rely upon government assistance to help displaced workers. As an example, the Economic Dislocation and Worker Adjustment Assistance Act (EDWAA) funds retraining courses for laid-off workers. Firms may cooperate in the delivery of state or federal programs, but many companies prefer to fund "in-house" outplacement services rather than work with the government. Even though laid-off workers would obtain more assistance from EDWAA and the firm could save substantial sums of money, many companies eschew government assistance because it brings public exposure.

WEIGHING THE EVIDENCE

Empirical research on joblessness concludes that several corporate practices and program interventions help laid-off workers find better jobs more quickly.[35] Among the more helpful strategies are:

- advance notice, which helps workers find jobs before the unemployment insurance and other benefits expire;

- severance pay and extended benefits that allow workers to avoid financial disasters and seek appropriate jobs;

- outplacement assistance that helps workers who often have little knowledge of how to look for work in today's labor market;

- alternatives to layoffs that minimize the damage for laid-off workers and those who remain;

- coordination of services and benefits between the firm and public-sector agencies so that those who are laid off receive the maximum available benefits and help in seeking employment.

Few private companies currently follow all these strategies, unless they are forced to abide by union contracts. During downsizing episodes, most corporations seek to ease the pain for laid-off workers rather than find a cure for what ails them. There are exceptions, however. Companies like General Electric, Duracell, and Stroh's Brewery have demonstrated that concern for laid-off individuals is not inconsistent with a concern for the economic vitality of their firms.[36]

The typical private-sector response is not surprising because it is a rational response to market forces. Companies want to minimize the negative perceptions held by remaining employees, political leaders, and the public at the lowest cost possible, but they are not interested in investing in new skills for laid-off workers, who may later help competitors. (The extent to which *government-sponsored* programs help the casualties of downsizing will be discussed in detail in Chapter 4.)

Do Companies Get What They Want from Downsizing?

From the perspective of private firms, layoffs are a mixed bag of positive and negative outcomes. Some firms find that staff reductions yield greater productivity, save money, increase market share, and preserve a smaller, but still loyal, workforce. Other firms report declining productivity, deteriorating quality, minimal savings, and a disgruntled workforce—and the more often these firms downsize, the worse the after-effects.[37] Whether the effort is regarded as positive or negative for the firm depends, in part, on what goals are set in the first place and, of course, how the layoffs are carried out.

Empirical research on corporate downsizing strongly suggests that many firms are doing a poor job of implementing cutbacks and are not achieving their goals. Consider the following evidence:

◆ Approximately half of the firms surveyed by the Wyatt corporation were successful in cutting costs after downsizing in 1991; 68 percent claimed success in 1993 (see Figure 2.3, page 104).

◆ Only one-third of the firms responding to AMA surveys from 1989 to 1994 reported increases in productivity following downsizing; only half reported increases in profits (see Figure 2.4, page 104).

◆ Fewer than half of the 1,468 firms surveyed in 1990 by the Society for Human Resources Management reported productivity gains after downsizing.[38]

◆ Only one-fourth of the firms that downsized in the late 1980s and early 1990s improved productivity, cash flow, or shareholder's return on investment, according to Arthur D. Little Company.[39]

◆ Only half of the 338 executives surveyed in 1993 reported quality improvements in the wake of downsizing.[40]

◆ Fewer than half of the 497 large companies in the United States and another 124 in Europe succeeded in their efforts to gain market share through corporate restructuring, according to a 1994 study by CSC Index, a consulting firm.[41]

◆ The most common approach to downsizing, "across-the-board—grenade-type approaches—is associated with organizational dysfunction," according to a comprehensive study of over 150 firms.[42]

"Most cost cutting actions do not remove work, only the people who do it," says Quinn Spitzer of Kepner-Tregoe. He describes the problem of controlling costs:

FIGURE 2.3
Percentage of Downsized
Firms Claiming Success

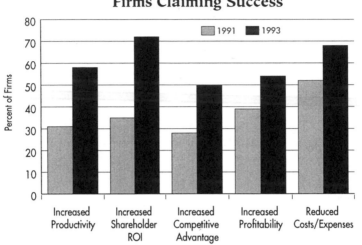

Source: Wyatt Company, *Best Practices in Corporate Restructuring: Wyatt's 1993 Survey of Corporate Restructuring* (Chicago, Ill.: The Wyatt Company, 1993), p. 4.

FIGURE 2.4
Effects of Downsizing on Operating Profits,
Productivity, and Employee Morale

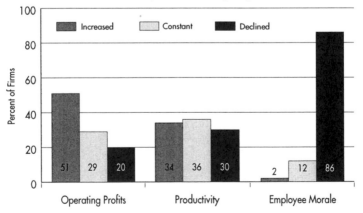

Source: American Management Association, *1994 AMA Survey on Downsizing and Assistance to Dislocated Workers*, p. 4.

> The heads roll and the compensation budget goes down. Stockholders and the investment community applaud. But because the work remains, costs eventually pop up in the form of "special" projects, or temporary help, or new hires.[43]

In fact, many businesses replace laid-off employees with part-time or contract workers.

Many companies boost hours toiled by remaining employees. One study reported that half of the companies that laid off employees extended working hours, paid more overtime, or both rather than hire new workers. In 1994, the average factory workweek averaged forty-two hours, including 4.6 hours of overtime, near a postwar high.[44] Within a year of laying people off, over half the firms refilled at least some of the positions.[45]

Greater profits is also a stated rationale for corporate downsizing, but again the record is disappointing. In 1991, one-third of the firms in the Wyatt survey accomplished this goal. Profits rose in 46 percent of the firms that undertook downsizing in 1993. Those profits were typically used to lower company debt, increase dividends to stockholders, and invest in new technologies that would probably lead to additional layoffs.[46] Obviously, some of the changes are due to the improving economy, illustrating the point that downsizing does not occur in an economic and market vacuum.

Stories of both successful and failed attempts to restructure corporations abound. Suffering from losses in sales and profits, Compaq Computer cut its workforce by one-third in 1991. Since then, sales and profits have tripled. Now employment has also increased above where it was before the downsizing started. Caterpillar cut its workforce by 31 percent, lowered its costs, and increased productivity and profits.[47] Although Bank of America reduced its workforce from 86,000 to 54,000, the remaining workforce is more productive than before.[48]

In contrast, Eastman Kodak chopped its workforce five times, eventually eliminating 12,000 jobs at a cost of $2.1 billion. After the first downsizing episode, profits increased by 63 percent, but then losses followed for six straight quarters. Profits tripled the following year, but then fell, and Kodak downsized again. Profit margins dropped by half, Kodak stock dropped, and "the bottom line is not much bigger than it was ten years ago."[49] Many factors were at work during this period, including an acquisition and the rise in the value of the U.S. dollar, but the experience with downsizing contributed to Kodak's woes.[50] Critics claim IBM lost billions because it failed to have a thoughtful human resource strategy for dealing with laid-off workers and those who remained with the firm.[51]

Increased productivity is another important goal of corporate downsizing decisions. In 1991, nearly three-quarters of the AMA survey respondents sought higher productivity, but only one in five succeeded. By 1995, one in three firms reported productivity increases after downsizing. Another survey, conducted in the same time frame, reported similar results.[52]

It is not uncommon for downsizing to hurt productivity, quality, and lead to other negative by-products. Some economists argue that downsizing strategies have gone too far, robbing companies of the needed research, development, and advertising and marketing staffs that generate new products and new market opportunities.[53] "You can't save your way to prosperity," explains Burke Stinson, spokesman for AT&T—a company well versed in the practice of large-scale work force reductions.[54] "This continuous downsizing—it's corporate anorexia. You can get thin, but it's not the way to get healthy," argues Gary Hammel, a British management consultant.[55]

THE SURVIVORS

Laid-off workers are not the only ones affected by downsizing. Managers must contend with the shock, hurt feelings, and lingering fear of those who remain with the firm.[56] These so-called survivors lose confidence in the firm and experience high stress levels and doubts about their futures.[57] They often seek more secure employment opportunities elsewhere.[58] Survivors are angry with management for causing the layoffs and mishandling them. They are fearful that the corporate axe may fall on them next. And remaining employees are often not prepared for their new roles in the firm.[59]

Eighty-six percent of the firms that participated in the 1994 AMA study of downsizing reported declines in employee morale (see Figure 2.4, page 104).[60] "Since there is so much employee distrust, there's an increase in . . . silent sabotage—workers aren't enthused about their jobs and putting in the effort they once did. There is a big turnoff at every level of corporate life," according to William J. Morin, CEO of Drake Beam Morin, a leading outplacement firm.[61]

Nearly one in three companies reported decreased productivity in the AMA surveys. A survey conducted by the Wyatt corporation found that more than half of downsizing firms experienced problems with motivation among employees; more than a third had problems keeping employees that they wanted to retain; and another 11 percent indicated greater attendance problems.[62]

Reshaping corporate cultures that evolved over decades is a very hard thing to do. Employees are not going to work harder for a firm that is no longer committed to them. White-collar and blue-collar workers alike feel insecure and threatened. The experiences at Pratt and Whitney in Connecticut are illustrative of the consequences of economic change. In a survey of 20,000 Pratt employees in July 1993, which was undertaken after a major layoff, 92 percent revealed that they frequently worried about the future of the company, and only 14 percent said they felt they had job security.[63]

An employee who survived two rounds of layoffs summarized the feelings of many workers: "How can we focus on problems when we don't even know whether or not we'll have a job next fall. It's very hard to be a team player if no one knows what the game is."[64] In a message to employees, Pratt and Whitney's president conceded that "levels of employee satisfaction at Pratt are substantially below even those organizations undergoing the most traumatic change."[65]

Maintaining a bond between workers and the firm is often paramount to success. The "neglect of human capital in the U.S." has undermined the strategic competitiveness of U.S. businesses.[66] Companies compete not only on efficiency but, increasingly, on service response time and quality. Mistrust and lack of commitment by workers often translates into an erosion of service quality vital to companies' success.[67] Companies also face a "brain drain" as the accumulated knowledge of able employees leave the firm. This is especially true when firms use attrition and early retirement strategies, because the most-able employees often use these opportunities to depart.

GAUGING THE RESULTS

Initially, management gurus claimed that downsizing was a "risk-free" endeavor.[68] Many firms still contend they can slash workforces with few negative consequences. If additional workers are needed, they can be obtained. "Just-in-time" manufacturing principles are being applied to human resource strategies.

Critics claim that companies are addicted to downsizing. The AMA study found that two-thirds of the companies that downsize do it again the following year.[69] Downsizing "allows CEOs and boards of directors to feel they have accomplished something."[70] Downsizing strategies often ignore the workforce skills, company loyalty, and employee stability that the firm needs to remain competitive over the long term. Downsizing is a "quick fix" to corporate woes that can cause damage years later.

UNIONS AND WORKER DISLOCATION

Over the last fifteen years, union workers have suffered more permanent job losses than any other group in the economy. Most of the over 4.1 millon U.S. manufacturing employees who permanently lost their jobs between 1979 and 1989 were union members.[71] Union members as a percent of all wage and salary employees declined from 26.5 percent to 15.5 percent between 1977 and 1994.[72]

With their membership and political power dwindling, unions have been on the defensive. Unions were able to convince Congress to enact WARN, the law governing advance notice, and several transitional training and cash transfer programs, but efforts aimed at preserving jobs for union workers through greater regulation and restrictive trade policies have failed. Federal government policy has supported free trade and rejected union entreaties for protection from foreign imports, except for the voluntary import quotas imposed on the Japanese auto industry. Despite an all-out effort, unions could not prevent the passage of the North American Free Trade Agreement (NAFTA) in 1993.

Unions have been more forceful in blunting the effects of economic change at the bargaining table. Through collective bargaining, unions have helped prevent layoffs and furnished substantial aid to former employees, including training and extended health benefits (see Figure 2.5). In 1980, collective bargaining agreements rarely included negotiated benefits for training assistance, but by 1988, more than one in four contracts had such provisions. Few had job search assistance provisions in 1980; by 1988, one in five offered this form of help.[73]

Over the past decade, contract negotiations demonstrated clear shifts in priorities among union leaders and members. Unions have traded off wage and benefit increases for job security. For many unions, the "wage concession" era of the 1980s also meant "stock-for-wage trade"—giving employees stock ownership.[74] Some unions have negotiated "no-layoff" clauses for those with the greatest seniority. Others have swapped greater job security for changes in work rules. For example, some contracts allow companies to employ part-time workers for jobs, as long as those union members who are presently laid-off are called back first.[75]

FIGURE 2.5
Percentage of Union Contracts Containing
Worker Assistance Provisions, 1980–1988

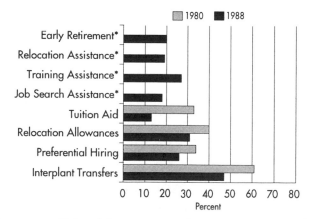

*The U.S. Department of Labor did not summarize these provisions in 1980 because of their infrequency.

Source: Wayne Vroman and Douglas Wissoker, *Alternatives for Managing Production Cutbacks: A Report to the National Commission for Employment Policy,* February 1990, pp. 34–36.

Union strategies also encompass a wide range of labor-management agreements for increasing productivity and efficiency while protecting workers' job security. Unions are working with employers to enhance industry competitiveness through training and team efforts with management.[76]

Although labor-management teams are multiplying, labor leaders remain skeptical. They fear that employers will use this tactic to bypass union representation. Examples of new labor-management partnerships include the United Steelworkers of America (USWA) and the major steel producers; the International Brotherhood of Electrical Workers and General Electric; the Communications Workers of America and several regional telephone operating companies; the Amalgamated Clothing and Textile Workers and Levi Strauss.[77]

Many union officials believe that the current trend in downsizing is aimed at undercutting unions to gain further wage concessions or eliminating unions altogether. This concern certainly seems justified when companies that have laid off permanent union workers then turn around after layoffs and replace previously internal functions with part-time workers, consultants, and others who are not union members. Some companies return to previous employment levels, but with a smaller percentage of union workers. These tactics are being contested in the auto industry.[78]

UNITED STEELWORKERS AND DISLOCATED WORKERS

The steel industry and its principal union, the United Steelworkers of America, illustrate effective union and management practices with respect to downsizing.[79] In addition to trying to prevent layoffs through import restrictions, the steelworkers' union has negotiated for greater worker adjustment assistance, including training, outplacement, and extended benefits and employee buyouts.

The USWA has extensive experience in dealing with layoffs. Over the last twenty years, as American mills modernized or closed, the domestic steel industry shed over 320,000 workers—more than half of the total workforce.[80] For instance, the Homestead Plant of the United States Steel Corporation, once the most famous steel mill in the world, employed over 30,000 workers in 1970, but by 1986 all of those jobs were eliminated.[81] The outdated production and rolling technology of the mill were replaced by the same cost-efficient methods used by foreign competitors.[82]

In 1983, the USWA negotiated Appendix O of the Steel Basic Labor Agreement, which requires companies to work jointly with the union to help displaced workers. The agreement contains several important features:[83] firms must give early notification of impending layoffs; each company contributes toward dislocated worker assistance funds; special programs are offered to individuals on "prolonged layoffs"; each plant forms a joint union-company advisory committee; and a dispute resolution system is established. The agreement recognizes the union's primary responsibility for pursuing federal job training funds.[84]

The USWA has a robust system for assisting dislocated steelworkers. Funded from several sources, including the steel companies, federal, state and local governments, USWA programs try to insure a seamless path from layoff to reemployment. For example, under USWA's Jump-Start Program,[85] USWA's Dislocated Worker Task Force sets up worker assistance programs with local union officials immediately after notice of an impending layoff. The task force applies for discretionary funding under Economic Dislocation and Worker Adjustment Assistance Act (EDWAA) and the Trade Adjustment Assistance Act (TAA). If government funds are not available, the union establishes a dislocated-worker center near the plant.

Since 1983, the USWA has channeled over $53 million of federal job training monies into programs for over 50,000 unemployed steelworkers.[86] In practice, approximately 25 percent of the discretionary funds available under EDWAA have been set aside for dislocated steelworkers since the program's inception.

The USWA programs are governed by several guiding principles.[87] The efforts of the union, company, and community are combined so that all employees at the affected plant, whether union members or not, receive assistance. The union is notified at least ninety days before a plant or unit closure. This allows for effective interventions before workers exhaust their unemployment insurance benefits.

Comprehensive services are made available to dislocated workers in one center or in satellite centers under the same management. The centers offer active job search assistance, such as seminars on résumé writing and interviewing skills, job clubs, and job search counseling. Basic skills and occupational training programs are also made available. Centers help dislocated workers start or develop their own businesses.

After more than ten years, the USWA has learned several lessons about helping dislocated workers. Laid-off workers often isolate themselves after a major plant closure and quickly become disheartened after a few weeks of an unsuccessful job searching. Therefore, peer counselors actively recruit workers into the dislocated worker centers. The USWA also believes that local unions should operate the centers instead of government, company, or private contractors.[88] Such arrangements give workers a stake in the program and improve participation.

SUMMARY

Corporate decisions about workforce size and how to handle layoffs directly affect the economic future of Americans. As corporations choose downsizing, thousands of workers are losing their jobs permanently every day. Driven by the need for short-term profits and concerns about competition, many firms have decided to "run lean." Beyond those who are directly affected by layoffs are millions of workers who worry about their futures.

Most laid-off workers are not likely to receive more than a few weeks of outplacement assistance and a modest severance payment from their former employers. Private firms may not have the resources and are not motivated to help those whom they have discarded. Responsibility for locating another job or obtaining new skills and the costs of economic transition must be borne by individuals or society.

Does the public interest dictate a different response? Government policymakers have been slow in responding to the massive changes in the economy. Current federal policy does little to inhibit layoffs. Even the early warning system that is supposed to give workers advance notice is weak and widely ignored. Indeed, many federal laws encourage corporate downsizing. Federal tax policy reduces the tax liability of firms that lay off workers. Businesses pay only a small increase in unemployment taxes when they cut jobs. (Federal and state government policies regarding dislocated workers are examined in Chapters 4 and 5, respectively.)

TRANSITION IN THE AUTOMOTIVE, TELECOMMUNICATIONS, AND DEFENSE INDUSTRIES

The three industries selected for closer inspection—automotive, telecommunications, and defense—represent a significant share of U.S. employment. Within these industries the forces transforming the American economy are all at work: new technology, international competition, the overhaul of manufacturing, deregulation, stock-driven corporate planning, and the changing U.S. role in the world.

Employment in these industries has plummeted rapidly this decade. Millions of skilled and semiskilled workers making middle-class wages were tossed out of their "permanent" jobs. While the telecommunications and automotive industries are both showing signs of increased revenues and profitability, the prognosis for employment in these industries is not bright: downsizing is likely to continue for the foreseeable future.

THE AUTOMOTIVE INDUSTRY

The U.S. auto sector suffered from many ills for many years, but after shedding hundreds of thousands of workers, it is once again increasing its market share and posting large profits. Whether or not the troubles are over, its problems over the past two decades have had profound effects on the U.S. economy and employment. One in seven domestic jobs is connected to the auto industry and one in eight tax dollars are paid by an auto industry employee.[1]

Since 1981, more than half a million automotive jobs have been eliminated.[2] Two years ago, the largest of the "big three" automakers, General Motors (GM), said it would eliminate another 75,000 jobs. GM is recovering from a $4.9 billion loss—the largest net loss in U.S. corporate history—posted in 1991. By 1993, it had turned around and had profits of $2.5 billion and by 1995 they grew to $6.9 billion.[3] GM is still the nation's single largest company, with 775,100 employees.[4] Thousands more workers in the automotive supply and manufacturing industry are dependent on GM contracts for their livelihood.

Since 1992, automakers have benefitted from excellent market conditions, the weak U.S. dollar, and voluntary limits on imports. As a result, U.S. firms postponed many scheduled plant shutdowns and layoffs. Of the twenty facilities targeted for shutdown by GM, only four have actually stopped producing cars. Most American automobile plants are operating at 100 percent capacity to meet increased demand. Rather than hire new workers, U.S. automakers have met the rising demand for cars and trucks by paying current workers record amounts in overtime pay.[5]

The prospects for U.S. auto workers are uncertain because the underlying problems that plagued American automakers in the 1970s and 1980s have not disappeared. Automakers and unions are still struggling for a formula that will allow them to remain profitable while fighting off stiff domestic and international competition. The U.S. share of worldwide motor vehicle production has declined from 24.8 percent in 1986 to 20.7 percent in 1992.[6] Massive layoffs and plant closings are part of the recipe for transforming the auto industry. Operating costs have dropped and productivity has increased—from twenty-two vehicles per worker in 1982 to thirty vehicles per worker in 1992.[7] U.S. autoworkers are the most productive in the world—about a third more productive than workers employed at Toyota or Mercedes-Benz.[8]

Two characteristics of the American automobile industry make it especially important. First, the industry employs millions of low-skilled workers and pulls them into the middle class through regular wage hikes. Historically, automakers have hired individuals with only a high school diploma or less. Workers did not need to be highly skilled because auto assembly lines minimized human input and error. Constructed around industrial management principles popular seventy years ago, production lines were not supposed to be staffed with well-trained craftspeople, but limited-purpose "human robots."

Second, labor unions have played a strong role in shaping the work conditions and the way layoffs are conducted in the automotive industry. Unionization of the auto industry was not just spurred by the desire for higher wages and benefits, but also by the concern for job security. Early union organizers feared that companies would lay off senior and more costly employees and replace them with people who earned less.

The automobile industry reflects the tension between traditional union demands for higher wages, benefits, and job security, and management's concern for productivity increases and profitability. Union leaders recognize the need for cooperative efforts that might restore U.S. competitiveness and protect U.S. market share.[9] They realize that lost market share in the U.S. auto industry goes "straight to Japanese-owned car plants in the U.S. or to imports."[10] If unions push too hard for job preservation and cause higher labor costs, American automakers may lose market share. If they don't fight for job security and worker rights, companies will be free to downsize at will and unions will be squeezed out of existence.

Labor and management are still sorting out their respective roles. Labor leaders are demonstrating their concern for the profitability of automakers while they work to protect members' jobs. Management increasingly regards workers as critical elements in making high quality cars that people will buy. Employee involvement, training and cooperative management are now hallmarks of the industry. Automakers want to avoid costly and hostile union confrontations.

In the late 1980s and early 1990s, "job security for the majority" and "layoff benefits" replaced "wage and benefit increases for all" as a centerpiece of the United Auto Workers (UAW) negotiation strategy.[11] Management gained greater efficiency through lower wage settlements. They also retained the ability to manipulate the size of the workforce as demand dictates. Unions gave management greater flexibility to increase productivity. Lower wages paid to new hires, for example, prevented losses to senior employees.[12]

The UAW has fought vigorously for job security and layoff benefits. Unlike other industries with weaker unions, layoffs in the auto industry are regulated through collective bargaining agreements. The current contracts with the "big three" automakers—GM, Ford, and Chrysler—reflect the successful advocacy of the unions. For example, the three-year contract signed in 1993 enhanced job security for workers. Under the agreement with Ford, which is similar to agreements with the other large companies, the union participates with the company in any decision to subcontract work to outside firms. The company is required to consider job security in any subcontracting decisions.[13]

In response to the union's tighter control over layoffs, managers fashioned new tactics to maintain control over the size of their workforce. One practice is known as "whipsawing." In this method, management announces impending layoffs, but leaves open for discussion which specific plants will be cut back or closed.[14] Thus, plants and local unions in one part of the country are pitted against those in other communities.

Layoff prevention through skills upgrading is also emphasized by the UAW and automakers. Chrysler and Ford fund extensive educational and skills-enhancement programs for their workers. Even if these training programs do not eliminate layoffs, they may at least shorten the duration of unemployment. Moreover, retraining workers may improve productivity during their future employment with the firm and reduce the benefits paid to former employees while they are seeking employment.

A joint UAW-Chrysler board oversees a National Training Center that funds training for the company's workforce. Local training committees, often located at the auto plants, maintain extensive training programs in such areas as computer skills.[15] Chrysler also furnishes tuition assistance of up to $1,250 annually for active employees engaged in personal enhancement, $1,800 annually for job-related courses, and up to $2,800 annually for academic courses. Since the inception of the tuition aid program in 1986, Chrysler has spent approximately $33 million providing over 100,000 educational vouchers to employees.[16]

Strict regulations govern how workers will be treated before, during, and after job cutbacks. People targeted for a layoff may transfer to other auto plants in order of seniority. Extensive severance and early retirement packages are offered to laid-off employees in accordance with union contracts.[17] Salaried workers who agree to quit may receive six to fifteen months of paid leave to search for employment elsewhere.[18] Unions drove up the costs of worker adjustment programs to make management pay a higher cost for downsizing. Even though the costs of providing these benefits are deductible against profits, corporate leaders are beginning to realize that there are limits to how far it is prudent to cut their workforce.

Continued downsizing has its dark side even for profitable auto makers. Chrysler now has "more retirees than active hourly people, and Ford is running so lean that it would have to replace each retiree with a new hire, and then it would be paying for a new worker as well as paying a retiree."[19]

When GM, Ford, or Chrysler closes a plant or initiates a layoff, they must provide at least six months notice and often notice is given two to five years ahead of time. Laid-off workers are guaranteed 95 percent of their prior salary for the first thirty-six weeks. These employers also provide $3,100 per year in tuition assistance for workers who attend vocational school or college. Individuals permanently laid off by Chrysler are given up to $6,000 annually for retraining costs.

If workers are still unemployed after thirty-six weeks, the automakers must provide 100 percent of salary and benefits to the individual for the length of the contract.[20] At this time, the former employee is either rehired for a job similar to the one held before, or placed in a nonprofit organization. These community jobs are subsidized until the worker either finds new work or is called back to work at the auto plant.[21] Approximately 22,000 GM workers benefitted from this provision between 1990 and 1993.[22]

In their 1993 contract settlements, the automakers also agreed to replenish the $1.1 billion income security fund that was utilized by laid-off workers, and to set aside an additional $600 million in reserve funds. The auto companies also agree to the formula which requires them to replace 50 percent of all workers who retire, quit, or die. Finally, the automakers agreed to establish new technical skills training programs for autoworkers.[23]

Critics charge that automakers manipulate layoffs to gain leverage in collective bargaining negotiations or to drive up stock values. The evidence is not conclusive, but it is likely that they use these techniques. As explained earlier, the stock market typically reacts positively to plant closings, layoffs, and other cost shaving strategies. But the positive movement is usually short-lived and value stabilizes at the level prior to the announcement or lower.[24]

THE TELECOMMUNICATIONS INDUSTRY

Widespread layoffs in the telecommunications industry began after the breakup of AT&T in the mid-1980s and came into full swing in the 1990s. AT&T, the largest telecommunications company in the world, with 309,000 employees and 1993 revenues of $37.2 billion, cut its workforce by over 100,000 in less than ten years.[25] Another 55,000 layoffs are promised over the next two years in AT&T's operations.[26]

AT&T was not alone in cutting its workforce (see Figure 3.1). Between June 1993 and January 1994, 85,100 jobs were eliminated in the telecommunications industry. Some of the major cuts included 16,000 at NYNEX, 17,000 at GTE, 10,000 at Pacific Telesis, and 9,000 at U.S. West.[27]

FIGURE 3.1
Telecommunications Industry Downsizing,
November 1992–February 1994

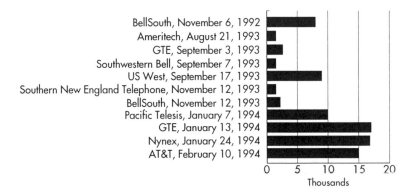

Source: Edmund Andrews, "AT&T Cutting Up to 15,000 to Trim Costs," *New York Times,* February 11, 1994, p. D1.

Telecommunications industry downsizing is driven by a number of factors, including changing technology and greater competition. In AT&T's case, labor force reductions initially stemmed from the reorganization following divestiture, which spun off local service to the "Baby Bells." Later, they were caused by breaking up the company into four business units.

Productivity-enhancing technology is another source of displacement among all telecommunications companies. Although productivity increased gradually over the life of the industry, this trend accelerated during the late 1980s and early 1990s, when thousands of back room office workers were replaced by computers and through job reorganizations.

New service-installation technologies and voice-recognition technology cost people thousands of permanent jobs.[28] For example, the eight transactions for an installation order are now handled by one individual who takes the order, sets up the account, and initiates telephone service. While this has eliminated in some cases one of every four jobs, it makes the remaining workers' skills even more critical because they must adapt to advancing technical applications. Computers that recognize voice commands will further reduce the need for operator-assisted services.[29]

Technological change stimulated an industry-wide trend in facility consolidations which, of course, lead to economic dislocation. In the near future, AT&T will abolish forty telephone operator centers in twenty-four states and create five centralized operations; GTE will knock out twenty-six of their thirty customer service centers in thirty states; U.S. West will merge 560 offices in fourteen states into ten urban centers and cut nearly one in five employees, or over 9,000 jobs.[30] In 1990, MCI consolidated seven of its field sales and marketing divisions into four.[31]

Industry competition contributes to cost-cutting and downsizing, while divestiture encourages the entrance of new, nonunion companies into the market. These new firms, such as MCI and Sprint, exert downward pressure on wages and benefits and are powerful driving forces for greater efficiency.[32] With rates for long-distance and cellular services falling in response to competition, companies constantly search for cost-cutting measures. As a by-product, the larger, older, and more bureaucratic firms—AT&T and GTE—were compelled to shed employees.

Consider the case of GTE—a firm that has delivered phone service in four states for thirty-three years. Over time, it became the least efficient telecommunications firm in the industry, when measured by number of employees per phone line.[33] Whereas the industry average is 265 phone lines per worker, GTE services only 200 lines per worker, and the industry leader, Bell Atlantic, handles 288 lines per employee.[34] As a result, GTE will cut 28,000 workers by 1997 in addition to the 24,000 jobs cut between 1988 and 1993.[35]

MCI, one of the fastest growing firms in the industry, differs vastly from its older competitors, AT&T, GTE, and Sprint. MCI entered the telecommunications business with a "lean" employment philosophy. Line managers were not allowed to hire as many staff as the typical AT&T business unit. MCI never entered regulated markets and therefore never developed the bureaucratic overhead that its competitors are now cutting.[36] Despite all of these advantages, MCI laid off 1,500 of its 25,000 employees in 1991.

MCI is currently expanding its workforce to enter new markets undergoing deregulation. According to its managers, MCI foresees no more layoffs. In fact, recent purchases of related companies are an effort to bolster its skilled workforce. Nevertheless, MCI's struggle to remain lean along with its competitors will continue.

Unions helped determine how layoffs are handled in the telecommunications industry, but they have not succeeded in gaining the same dominant position occupied by the UAW in the auto industry. Not surprisingly, planned layoffs have created significant tension between labor and management. The Communications Workers of America (CWA) and the International Brotherhood of Electrical Workers (IBEW) insist, pursuant to union regulations, that workers with the most seniority should have the greatest job security. Management complains that such practices are unfair to younger, more highly qualified workers and that it hurts productivity. Management wants to retain only those with the best employment records and highest qualifications.

Despite these conflicts, labor and management have cooperated during the restructuring of the industry. The most enduring example is the Alliance for Employee Growth and Development (hereafter the Alliance), established in 1986 by AT&T, CWA, and the IBEW as a result of collective bargaining. The Alliance furnishes career counseling, skills training, tuition assistance, financial planning, relocation counseling, preretirement planning, and placement assistance to over 70,000 AT&T workers and all laid-off employees affiliated with the CWA or IBEW.

The Alliance's $25 million budget for 1993 was based on a formula whereby AT&T contributes around $10 per employee every month. It is managed by two executive directors—one appointed by AT&T, the other by the unions. The eight-person board of trustees consists of four executives from AT&T and four top-level union leaders, including the two international presidents. The 315 local operating units of the Alliance, called Alliance Local Committees, are responsible for assessing employee needs.[37] Staff cite the decentralized structure and "employee-driven" culture of the Alliance as a principal reason for the program's acceptance among workers.[38] The Alliance recently spun off a for-profit consulting group called Alliance Plus. It offers consulting services to corporations, labor unions, and public and private agencies.

AT&T employees facing layoff are to receive at least sixty-days notice under the federally mandated provision of the Worker Adjustment and Retraining Notification Act (WARN). More commonly, however, they learn of impending cutbacks one or two years in advance. At the time of notice, employees are apprised of services available through the Alliance, and company severance payments and government-funded unemployment insurance benefits are detailed.

All workers targeted for layoff engage in career planning exercises. Individuals undergo skills and aptitude tests and then work with career counselors who help them choose the most practical career paths. Job searches for positions within the corporation are also conducted. If a permanent job cannot be found, many individuals receive part-time or temporary jobs with the company or additional help in finding employment. Employees may also obtain skills training that will help them get a job with AT&T or elsewhere. Government-funded literacy education grants and federal dislocated worker programs are also utilized by the Alliance.

The challenges of economic transition and competition led CWA, the IBEW, and AT&T to enter into a "Workplace of the Future" agreement in 1992. It established joint union-management teams at workplace, business unit, and corporate levels. The agreement decentralizes and broadens decisionmaking about employment levels.[39]

GTE's approach to downsizing is still evolving. Management and the unions have not yet agreed on the appropriate mix of outplacement, retraining, and other services. Workers have been laid off without receiving outplacement benefit packages. GTE is now considering retaining Alliance Plus to handle its downsizing program.

In the coming years, new technologies and changing consumer preferences will produce cutbacks in some parts of the telecommunications industry and growth in others. For example, in 1990 there were 10 million cellular subscribers; today there are 30 million subscribers. In five years it may reach 60 million.[40] While telecommunications companies slash employment in their traditional long-distance telephone units, employment in the wireless companies is rising rapidly. MCI announced in 1994 that it will hire several thousand people for its wireless division, while laying off employees in other business units.[41]

THE DEFENSE INDUSTRY

During the 1980s, the defense industry experienced unprecedented growth. Defense spending grew 7.5 percent in real terms between 1981 and 1986. The Reagan administration's commitment to boosting defense spending meant a windfall in business for defense firms throughout the country. The nation aggressively expanded its storehouse of military hardware. For example, the Navy signed contracts to build several hundred ships;[42] spending on military aircraft jumped 75 percent in Reagan's first term over the level in the Carter administration;[43] the B-1 bomber and its producer, Rockwell International, were reinvigorated.

An array of high technology weapons systems were developed or deployed. The Pentagon initiated the F-117 "stealth" fighter at the Lockheed Corporation and the B-2 bomber was started at Northrop. The satellite-based missile defense system, known as "Star Wars," spread contracts to dozens of high-technology firms. Sophisticated research and development projects came with high price tags and huge increases in employment for high-technology firms and highly skilled scientists, engineers, and craftspeople. The influx of federal funds enabled defense firms to acquire talented, technically trained employees, and pay them well.

When the cold war abruptly ended after the collapse of the Soviet Union, federal spending declined sharply for military technology, weapons systems, and military bases. At the height of the Reagan buildup, defense spending accounted for 6.5 percent of the gross domestic product (GDP)—it is expected to be 3.3 percent of the GDP by 1998.[44]

When the military expenditures faded, people lost their jobs (see Figure 3.2). In just five years (fiscal years 1989 to 1994), over 1.4 million jobs were cut from the defense sector of the economy.[45] By way of comparison, the steel industry lost 250,000 jobs in twenty years.[46] More than 3.2 million defense-related workers may be dislocated between fiscal years 1992 and 1998.[47] While the defense industry only represents 5 percent of U.S. employment, it has endured 25 percent of the dislocations in the 1990-1991 recession.[48]

Employee dislocations in the defense industry were not caused by global market competition, the proliferation of high technology, or corporate profiteering. Defense dislocations happened because companies lost their only customer—the U.S. military. Most military technology is protected by federal law and defense firms are prohibited from selling their goods to other countries.

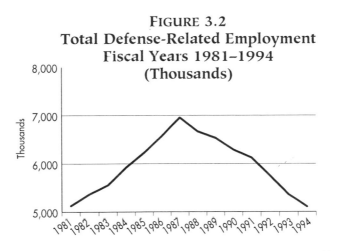

FIGURE 3.2
Total Defense-Related Employment
Fiscal Years 1981–1994
(Thousands)

Source: U.S. Department of Defense, *National Defense Estimates for FY 95,* Table 7–7.

No one else can buy a F-14 fighter or a Seawolf submarine. Most defense firms cannot replace their lost business with other customers. Only with the permission of the U.S. government can U.S. defense firms sell defense technology overseas, and whenever such an option arises, it invariably causes a heated political discussion.

Consider the Electric Boat Division of General Dynamics, which produces submarines at its Groton, Connecticut facility. At the Navy's request, Electric Boat was a single-product company.[49] In 1992 Electric Boat employed 21,500 people; however, defense cutbacks will eliminate all but 5,000 jobs in a few years.[50] As the largest employer in the region, the cuts to Electric Boat will devastate the local economy. The company predicts that the community will lose one private-sector job for every job eliminated at its facility.[51]

Electric Boat's story is by no means an isolated tale. In Atlanta, Lockheed cut 5,600 workers; in Los Angeles, Hughes Missile Systems laid off 6,000 people; in St. Louis, McDonnell-Douglas eliminated 11,000 positions; in Seattle, Boeing dropped off 31,000 people; in Dallas-Ft. Worth, General Dynamics laid off 10,000 employees.[52]

Clearly, some states are feeling the effects of defense cutbacks more than others. California, Massachusetts, and Connecticut will be particularly hard hit. Eighteen percent of all defense purchases came from California, for example.[53] In contrast, states like New Jersey were not heavily dependent on the defense dollar. In fiscal year 1992, defense spending accounted for 4 percent of the state's economic activity: the national average was 5.3 percent.[54] That year, 117,000 people, or 3.2 percent of the state's workforce, were employed in defense-related firms: the national average was 4.1 percent.[55] Companies in the state supplied only 2.3 percent of defense department hardware.[56]

Nevertheless, even states without heavy concentrations of the defense industry will find the transition to a peacetime economy difficult. Between fiscal years 1992 and 1998, 40,000 New Jersey defense workers may lose their jobs permanently.[57] Especially damaging is the decision to close the Philadelphia Naval Yard, which draws nearly half of its 7,000 workforce from New Jersey.[58] It is expected that another 35,000 support and subcontractor positions will be abolished.

There has never been a widespread reduction in U.S. defense spending of the magnitude created by the end of the cold war. Some cutbacks happened after the Vietnam War, but the civilian workers in defense industry did not experience layoffs of the size that are occurring in the 1990s. When confronted with layoff decisions, most companies fulfilled only the minimum requirements for notifying their workers. For example, Electric Boat, Martin Marietta, Boeing, GE Aerospace, and Grumman let employees know sixty days ahead of their layoff, as mandated by federal law. And unlike automakers and telecommunications firms, defense employers are not furnishing much in the way of training or other assistance to those who are separated from the firm.

This seeming disinterest in the future of dislocated workers is not surprising. Many of the firms are in desperate financial situations and have little hope of ever hiring people back. Moreover, collective bargaining agreements in the industry could not protect workers from the elimination of government contracts. If the government no longer purchases submarines, there is little the company can do about it. It is not analogous to the use of the telephone or the purchase of a car. For automakers, the question is how many people are to be employed in making cars, and in what country. For submarine manufacturers, the question is binary—either they make them, or they do not.

Martin Marietta's experience with defense cutbacks and employee layoffs illustrates some of the problems confronting workers and firms. In 1988, the company employed over 14,000 at its Colorado headquarters; by the end of 1994, employment was expected to plunge to 6,000.[59] The corporation notified workers only sixty days prior to a layoff. When management recognized the trauma associated with worker dislocation, they formed an internal task force to examine the way the company notifies its employees.

After several months, the company's task force recommended increasing the sixty-day notice. It argued that longer notice would help people adjust spending habits or delay major purchases, such as a new car. Not surprisingly, the task force found that layoffs severely affected the morale and dedication of the employees who remained with the firm. Finally, the task force said that greater advance notice would leave a more positive impression of the company with employees and in the communities where its facilities are located.

Senior management rejected the task force's recommendations. Citing legal and financial problems, they stuck with the minimal sixty-day notification. But the official corporate policy has been ignored by some plant managers, who are giving their workers information about layoffs in advance of the official notice date. These managers realize the positive impact of longer notification periods on those who are leaving and those who remain on the payroll.[60]

Due to the severe retrenchment in the defense sector, companies have no incentive to help workers retrain themselves for another industry or career. Most companies set up "career centers," which provide basic assistance on résumé writing and job hunting tips. Boeing Corporation provides unemployment workshops, career counseling, and interview skills training, but no retraining assistance.[61] The exception to this general pattern occurs when firms enter new markets and need to retrain employees. For example, Newport News Naval Shipyard in Virginia is hiring and retraining some former Philadelphia Naval Yard employees for work on civilian vessels.[62]

Given the minimal assistance provided by private firms and unions, laid-off defense workers and defense companies are turning to governments for help in making the transition to new careers. Often, former defense workers must find work in new industries, and they frequently require substantial retraining before entering new careers. Most large defense companies draw on federal "defense conversion" funds for the costs associated with training and layoffs. (For a more detailed description of these programs, see Chapter 4.)

Studies of worker retraining programs for defense workers have not been encouraging. The Rutgers' Project on Regional and Industrial Economies, for example, followed the 15,000 or so McDonnell Douglas workers who have lost their jobs in the St. Louis area since 1989. This study found that two years after being laid off, 64 percent had obtained new jobs, but a third of these had experienced pay cuts of $5,000 or more. The authors of the report, Michael Oden and Ann Markusen, criticized the Economic Dislocation and Worker Adjustment Assistance (EDWAA) program for failing to provide a timely and adequate response to the needs of laid-off defense workers. They were especially critical of the lack of income support, beyond unemployment insurance, and the limited use of on-the-job and other more intensive forms of retraining.[63]

Some firms are relying on state-funded programs. In Connecticut, for example, Electric Boat utilizes the state's "Rapid Response" team. State labor officials provide a four-hour seminar for notified workers on the benefits that are available. The seminar covers how employees can continue health benefits, obtain unemployment insurance, and cope with creditors.[64]

The causes of defense unemployment affect the future prospects of many employees. Defense workers have not been dislocated by global competition or advances in technology. Due to the highly technical nature of the research and development conducted by defense contractors, laid-off defense workers are one of the most highly skilled groups of American workers. It may not be necessary for some workers to upgrade their skills. Rather, they may have to learn entirely new skills or find an entirely new industry in which to practice their trade. Unfortunately, their skills and experience may have little applicability in corporations performing civilian work.

The problem is exacerbated by the number of unemployed defense workers who are looking for work in the same labor markets. It will take many years for 3 million unemployed defense workers to be completely reintegrated into the economy.[65] Many defense workers will find it difficult to replace the high income levels they enjoyed in the defense industry, in part because the largest portion of these job losers will be comprised of laborers and similarly skilled workers, who have a low level of educational attainment.[66]

4

FEDERAL PROGRAMS TRY TO CUSHION THE BLOW

Since the Great Depression of the 1930s, unemployment has been recognized as a problem requiring federal government intervention. When millions of Americans lost their jobs and had no government-sponsored safety net, Franklin Roosevelt and the Congress authorized temporary job programs and a system of unemployment insurance (UI). While job creation programs have since passed in and out of political favor, unemployment insurance has become one of the rock solid components of the American-style welfare state.

U.S. public policy treats unemployment largely as it did sixty years ago, when unemployment insurance began. Few modifications to the original package of benefits have been made since then. Unemployment insurance was, and still is, based on the premise that joblessness is temporary. Through employer and employee contributions, the government furnishes short-term, partial income support to help people bridge periodic gaps in employment.

Although unemployment insurance appropriately addressed unemployment for several decades after its enactment, it no longer meets the needs of many unemployed Americans. Unemployment insurance does not even cover a majority of unemployed workers. Americans are remaining unemployed for longer periods and many have permanently lost their jobs. Temporary income support is not sufficient for the long-term unemployed and it does nothing to upgrade the quality of the workforce.

Despite repeated debates over the inadequacies of the unemployment insurance system, there has been little change in the overall menu of services for the unemployed. Unemployment insurance is still the dominant program, consuming about 90 percent of the $31 billion in federal unemployment resources in fiscal year 1995.

The special problems of *displaced workers* were only recognized as distinct policy concerns in the last decade or so. Today there are four major displaced worker programs costing over $3.8 billion. These programs (see Figure 4.1, pages 132–133) are:

◆ Trade Adjustment Assistance Act (TAA)

◆ Economic Dislocation and Worker Adjustment Assistance Act (EDWAA), Title III of the Job Training Partnership Act (JTPA)

◆ Economic Assistance and Conversion (EAC), commonly referred to as "defense conversion"

◆ Adjustment Assistance to Workers Dislocated by the North American Free Trade Agreement (AANAFTA)

This chapter reviews and assesses these major federal programs along with unemployment insurance. Employment and training programs for low-income, unemployed workers, young workers, and welfare recipients are not covered here. Also not considered are smaller programs, such as those designed to help workers affected by the Clean Air Act amendments of 1990, or natural disasters, such as earthquakes.

What Are the Goals?

The main goal of federal unemployment programs is temporary financial aid. The programs are inflexible in that one cannot get help unless one has already been employed for a substantial period. Unemployment benefits are regarded as an insurance system into which working Americans pay as a hedge against future unemployment. These programs represent social insurance, not a

contract between workers and the government that implies mutual obligations.

Unemployment benefits are an entitlement, with few strings
attached. Once recipients qualify for these benefits, they face few
requirements in the UI system. People are required to look for
work, but there is no army of government officials monitoring
their behavior. In welfare programs, by contrast, recipients are
closely watched by government case workers, and recipients are
increasingly required by law to attend school or training classes
or to work in community jobs in return for assistance.

As currently administered, most federal unemployment programs are *passive* interventions. They are not geared toward finding the unemployed jobs or to enhancing their skills. Instead,
income support is provided during a period of idleness. Few
requirements are placed on the unemployed and, likewise, the programs do not intervene strongly or directly in the practices and
policies of the nation's business community.

Federal unemployment programs do no more than react to
unemployment, applying the temporary balm of cash payments,
with little effort devoted to prevention. When all cash transfer
components of the various unemployment programs are totaled,
they represent more than 95 percent of all federal spending for
unemployed workers.

Despite the similarities in overall goals, some important distinctions can be drawn among the five programs. The most important distinction is between *cash transfers* and *job search and
training programs.* Cash transfer programs dispense income to the
cyclically unemployed until they find new employment. Job search
and training programs aid dislocated workers by finding them jobs
or by preparing them for new jobs through skills training. It is
assumed that citizens in the latter program will reduce the likelihood of future unemployment by brushing up on their skills or by
learning a new trade.

CASH TRANSFERS

Intended as a stop-gap measure to assist recipients until they
find new employment, *unemployment insurance*, the largest federal
program for unemployed workers, targets individuals after they have
been laid off. Its sole purpose is to provide cash benefits to individuals

Figure 4.1
Principal Federal Programs Designed to Help Long-Term Unemployed Adults, Fiscal Year 1994

Program (Year of Initiation)	Fiscal Year 1994 Expenditures	Description	Target Group	Method	Approach
Unemployment Insurance (1935)[1]	$34 billion	PURPOSE: Partial and temporary income support; length and amount of benefits vary by state and by prior experience and wages of worker. Source: State tax levied on payrolls, financed by employers and employees. USE: Cash payments for twenty-six weeks unless extended by Congress.	Unemployed, laid off from regular job	Cash transfer	Passive
Trade Adjustment Act (1975)[2]	$189.9 million	PURPOSE: Temporary income support beyond the UI program and some training efforts. Source: Entitlement funded from general revenues. USE: Cash payments extending UI; some training efforts.	Unemployed due to import competition	Cash transfer and retraining	Passive
EDWAA (1982)[3]	$1.1 billion	PURPOSE: Provides training and related service for dislocated workers who are permanently displaced from their jobs, but are not necessarily poor or unskilled. SOURCE: Annual appropriations through the DoL's budget. USE: Training and cash grants. Twenty percent of funds are administered by the U.S. DoL and reserved for national activities including a discretionary grant program. Eighty percent of funds allocated to states for local and state projects.	Individuals or groups who have lost their jobs or have been notified of future layoff and are unlikely to return to their previous industry or position.	Training	Passive

PROGRAM (YEAR OF INITIATION)	FISCAL YEAR 1994 EXPENDITURES	DESCRIPTION	TARGET GROUP	METHOD	APPROACH
Defense—Worker and Community Assistance Programs (1992)[4]	$1.545 billion	PURPOSE: Ease the transition for personnel and communities as defense-dependence declines. SOURCE: Annual appropriations through DoD, DoC, DoE, and DoL. USE: Provides training and cash grants to former defense workers who have become dislocated due to military downsizing or industrial reductions; further offers assistance to communities who have been hard-hit by downsizing.	Former military personnel and industry employees, and affected communities	Training and cash transfer	Passive
Defense—TRP (1992)[5]	$404 million	PURPOSE: Provide high technology jobs for former defense workers and military personnel. Preserve defense industrial base. SOURCE: Annual appropriations to DoD. USE: Funding grants provided to encourage organizations to channel their research into commercial products and to improve the productivity of U.S. companies. Projects are funded in technological development, technological deployment, and manufacturing education and training.	Defense-dependent companies; universities and colleges	Technological investment	Passive and preventative
NAFTA (1993)[6]	$43.4 million	PURPOSE: Assist workers dislocated due to the "job flight" effects of NAFTA. SOURCE: Entitlement funds funneled through TAA, discretionary component funneled through EDWAA. USE: Provides cash transfer assistance to workers after dislocation.	Workers dislocated due to the effects of NAFTA	Cash transfer and retraining	Passive

1 CRS Issue Brief, Unemployment Compensation and Proposals for Reform, February 1, 1994; OMB, United States Budget FY 1993, February 1, 1994; OMB, United States Budget FY 1994.
2 Congressional Quarterly Almanac 1991–1994; CRS Issue Brief, Job Training Legislation and Budget Issues, March 14, 1994.
3 CRS Issue Brief, Training for Dislocated Workers Under the Job Training Partnership Act, December 3, 1992; CRS Issue Brief, Job Training Legislation and Budget Issues.
4 FY 1990 Defense Authorization Act; CRS Issue Brief, Defense Industry in Transition: Issues and Options for Congress, February 15, 1992; Congressional Budget Office, Reemploying Defense Workers: Current Experiences and Policy Alternatives, 1992; U.S. Congress, National Defense Authorization Act for Fiscal Year 1995, 1994, report 103-499.
5 CRS Issue Brief, Defense Technology Base Programs and Defense Conversion; Congressional Budget Office, The Technology Reinvestment Project: Integrating Military and Civilian Industries, 1992.
6 CRS Report for Congress, Adjustment Assistance for Workers Dislocated by the North American Free Trade Agreement, January 25, 1994; CRS Issue Brief, Job Training Legislation and Budget Issues.

for up to twenty-six weeks. During periods of high unemployment, Congress may also authorize "Emergency Extensions," adding twenty-six or more weeks, funded from federal resources.

The *Trade Adjustment Assistance Act*, created in 1975, helps workers who have been laid off by firms adversely affected by foreign trade. Initially, TAA offered supplemental income above the basic UI benefits. Now, however, TAA benefits are equal to UI benefits and are not made available until after individuals exhaust their UI benefits. TAA also retrains and refers participants to new jobs. Thus, a person enrolled in TAA can receive twenty-six weeks of UI, twenty-six weeks of TAA aid and, if enrolled in training, another twenty-six weeks of income assistance. Training has been stressed by policy makers and mandated for all enrollees since 1988.[1] Nevertheless, the cash transfers still represent approximately two of every three TAA dollars spent in fiscal year 1995. Liberal use of waiver provisions resulted in as many as half of the TAA recipients not receiving training.[2]

Adjustment Assistance to Workers Dislocated by the North American Free Trade Agreement was added to NAFTA in 1993 as part of a political compromise to win approval for the agreement in the House of Representatives. AANAFTA pays cash and training grants to workers who lose their jobs due to the effects of "job flight" resulting from NAFTA. While in the long-run NAFTA may improve employment possibilities in the U.S., its opponents complain that NAFTA will reduce employment in certain sectors of the U.S. economy such as textiles and manufacturing, particularly in the border states. Unlike UI, AANAFTA expenditures will be equally divided between cash transfers and retraining programs in Fiscal Year 1995.

In 1992, Congress passed the *Economic Adjustment and Conversion Act*. More commonly known as defense conversion assistance, the EAC has many goals—cash transfer and retraining for the unemployed and investments in new technologies. Individuals, companies, and communities will get help in making the difficult transition from a defense economy to a civilian-based economy.

EAC legislation gives cash grants to former defense employees, both civilian and military. Amounting to approximately two out of every three dollars spent through EAC, the grants have taken a number of different forms, including extension of health benefits for dislocated military personnel; grants to encourage early separation from active duty, national guard, and reserve service; and full pensions extended to military personnel separated five years prior to the normal achievement of full pension benefits.[3]

About 12 percent of every dollar spent in fiscal year 1995 will go toward retraining programs. EAC legislation authorizes training programs for former defense personnel, including Troops to Teachers, in which military personnel are encouraged to become teachers;[4] Department of Defense Environmental Scholarships, for military personnel who are willing to pursue a career in environmental restoration and hazardous waste management; and many general job and occupational assistance training courses, such as résumé writing.[5] Another goal of EAC is to assist those communities significantly affected by defense downsizing, providing economic planning and development assistance. Finally, the EAC legislation is responsible for the Technology Reinvestment Program (TRP), which is intended to preserve America's technological industrial base and generate "high end" technology jobs for future generations by providing technical assistance and financial support to companies attempting to convert defense production facilities to new product development.[6]

JOB SEARCH AND RETRAINING PROGRAMS

Created in 1982 as part of the Job Training Partnership Act, the Economic Dislocation and Worker Adjustment Assistance Act assists those unlikely to return to their previous jobs. EDWAA supports job search and training services that help dislocated workers find a job, improve their skills, or acquire new skills. EDWAA also supplies income support for individuals who cannot afford to enroll in training programs (although needs-based payments are received by less than 10 percent of those enrolled in the program). Approximately 50 percent of EDWAA resources are dedicated to retraining programs. The balance is used for administration and for job search assistance workshops and other forms of skills upgrading.

HOW MUCH FUNDING IS AVAILABLE?

Because unemployment insurance fluctuates with overall unemployment, government spending rises and falls with periods of growth and stagnation in the economy (see Table 4.1 for a six-year funding history). Between 1990 and 1992, when the recession deepened, unemployment insurance grew from $20.1 billion to $41.2 billion.[7] By 1993, the program had begun to decline, and is expected to drop below $27.2 billion in 1996.[8]

The budgetary significance of unemployment insurance is clear. In fiscal year 1992, when UI spending peaked, it comprised 97.7 percent of all federal unemployment funding. In fiscal year 1995, that percent is expected to drop to 87.6 percent. The growth in discretionary programs, such as EDWAA, and the creation of the EAC, TRP, and AANAFTA programs during this period demonstrate the rising importance of long-term unemployment to federal policy makers.

Another picture of federal funding trends is available through the total amount spent on programs other than UI (see Figure 4.2).

TABLE 4.1
Federal Program Funding, Fiscal Year 1990–1995
($Billions)

	1990	1991	1992	1993	1994	1995[1]
Unemployment Insurance[2]	$20.1	$28	$41.2	$39.2	$31	$27.2
Trade Adjustment Act[3]	$.1507	$.2695	$.2262	$.211	$.1899	$.231
EDWAA[4]	$.4636	$.527	$.527	$.5166	$1.1	$1.46
Defense—Worker and Community Assistance[5]	$0	$.2	$.2	$1.112	$1.545	$1.517
Defense—TRP[6]	$0	$0	$0	$.505	$.404	$.585
AANAFTA[7]	$0	$0	$0	$0	$.0135	$.0434
Annual Total		$20.714	$28.996	$42.153	$41.544	$34.252

[1] All FY 1995 figures represent the Clinton administration's funding request.
[2] CRS Issue Brief, Unemployment Compensation and Proposals for Reform, February 1, 1994; OMB, United States Budget FY 1993, February 1, 1994; OMB, United States Budget FY 1994.
[3] Congressional Quarterly Almanac 1991–1994; CRS Issue Brief, Job Training Legislation and Budget Issues, March 14, 1994.
[4] CRS Issue Brief, Training for Dislocated Workers Under the Job Training Partnership Act, December 3, 1992; CRS Issue Brief, Job Training Legislation and Budget Issues.
[5] FY 1990 Defense Authorization Act; CRS Issue Brief, Defense Industry in Transition: Issues and Options for Congress, February 15, 1992; Congressional Budget Office, Reemploying Defense Workers: Current Experiences and Policy Alternatives, 1992; U.S. Congress, National Defense Authorization Act for Fiscal Year 1995, 1994, report 103-499.
[6] CRS Issue Brief, Defense Technology Base Programs and Defense Conversion; Congressional Budget Office, The Technology Reinvestment Project: Integrating Military and Civilian Industries, 1992.
[7] CRS Report for Congress, Adjustment Assistance for Workers Dislocated by the North American Free Trade Agreement, January 25, 1994; CRS Issue Brief, Job Training Legislation and Budget Issues.

By fiscal year 1995, EDWAA is projected to grow by over 300 percent, from $463.6 million in 1990 to $1.46 billion in 1995. Funding for defense conversion has also risen sharply. In fiscal year 1991, $200 million was spent on worker and community assistance after the Defense Authorization Bill was amended to cover additional responsibilities.[9] Known as the Mavroules Amendment (named for Representative Nicholas Mavroules of Massachusetts), the law significantly expanded the scope of existing programs to help those adversely affected by reductions in defense activities. The amendment provides government funds from the Department of Defense for easing worker transition, promoting planning, and reducing adverse affects.[10] By 1994, overall EAC program funding is expected to grow to $4.9 billion,[11] of which $1.6 billion is slated for worker and community assistance programs. The Clinton administration has announced its intention to spend $22 billion on defense conversion through fiscal year 1997.[12]

The two trade-related programs, TAA and AANAFTA, are relatively small programs. TAA funding has remained relatively stable over the last several years, and AANAFTA is projected to grow only to $43 million in 1995.[13]

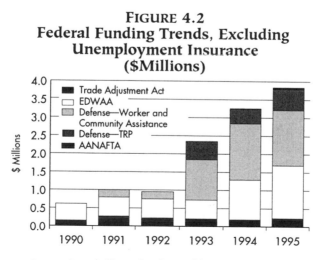

FIGURE 4.2
Federal Funding Trends, Excluding Unemployment Insurance ($Millions)

Source: Compiled by author from Table 4.1.

ENTITLEMENT AND DISCRETIONARY PROGRAMS

An important distinction must be drawn between entitlement and discretionary programs. Entitlements provide open-ended funding. If a person meets the criteria established by law, then that person receives the benefits, with no cap on federal spending. Discretionary programs receive annual Congressional appropriations, and thus Congress controls spending: politically popular programs succeed, unpopular ones falter.

Unemployment insurance is an entitlement funded through state taxes levied on payrolls. The revenue collected from these taxes is deposited with the U.S. Treasury and counted as federal revenue.[14] The Treasury credits each state's account in the Unemployment Trust Fund for the revenue received, and these credits establish federal spending authority to reimburse states for their UI benefit payments without the necessity of obtaining annual appropriations.

Like UI, TAA is funded as an entitlement; however, eligibility is determined by administrative judgments about the impacts of trade, so it is less of an economic barometer. While TAA funding may rise or fall year to year as the number of eligible recipients increases or decreases, the number of eligible trade-dislocated workers in any given year is relatively consistent. Therefore, funding fluctuations are modest.

Because EDWAA and EAC are funded through annual Congressional appropriations, their growth over the last several years reflects growing political support for worker adjustment programs. EDWAA and EAC increased faster than practically any other discretionary program. This is impressive in an era when Congress has imposed "hard-freezes" on domestic discretionary spending. Increases for these programs were funded by cutting others.

The priorities of the Clinton administration are reflected in the huge increases in EDWAA from 1990 to 1995, and in its proposals to overhaul the UI system. The Clinton administration argues that the federal government should fight unemployment by upgrading the skills of the workforce. The Republican-controlled Congress, elected in November 1994, however, is less supportive of training and education funding and plans to cut discretionary programs by 20 percent or more over the next five years.

AANAFTA has an entitlement component funded under a formula modeled after TAA and created by adding a new section to the Trade Act of 1974. It also has a discretionary component, established under the Job Training Partnership Act.[15] The entitlement side provides training and cash payments to anyone who meets the program's eligibility requirements, but training funds are capped at $80 million. The discretionary side is incorporated into national activities of the EDWAA and is funded through annual appropriations under the Department of Labor.

WHO IS ELIGIBLE?

The federal government utilizes a triad of requirements to calculate eligibility for unemployment programs. These criteria concern the unemployed worker's economic status, the worker's specific firm, and the industry from which the worker has been displaced. It is important to note that none of the programs reviewed here is based on financial need (see Figure 4.3, page 140).

These requirements can be compared to the operation of a series of filters. The first filter is unemployment insurance. With the least restrictions of any unemployment program, many Americans with prior work experience qualify. Those who are not from industries covered by the insurance system and people discharged for misconduct or who voluntarily resign are not eligible for assistance.

As the filters progress, more restrictions are added and fewer people qualify. Under EDWAA, eligible individuals are those who have lost their jobs or have received notice of impending layoffs (who are eligible for unemployment insurance) and are unlikely to return to their previous job or occupation.

The last few filters are made up of eligibility requirements for TAA, EAC, and AANAFTA, which restrict benefits to those affected by trade or defense policies.[16] Laid-off workers may qualify because they worked in a specific plant or factory that is slated for closure or large-scale layoff. When this happens, *and* federal officials approve funds for that business, workers who have lost jobs can get help.

Complex eligibility criteria are difficult to apply and they often confuse unemployed workers, employers, and even program administrators. Some of the criteria are difficult to apply in practice. How

FIGURE 4.3
Eligibility Criteria for Major Federal Programs

PROGRAM	ELIGIBILITY
Unemployment Insurance established by the Social Security Act of 1935	Any jobless worker who has sufficient work experience that meets the minimum requirements set by their state. Individuals are disqualified if job loss is due to: discharge for job-related misconduct; voluntary job separation; or a refusal of suitable employment.[1]
Job Training Partnership Act amended, Title III, Economic and Worker Adjustment Assistance Act of 1988	Individuals or groups who have lost their jobs or have received notice of impending layoffs, who are eligible for Unemployment Insurance, and are unlikely to return to their previous industry or job. Also, self-employed individuals (farmers) whose job loss results from economic conditions or natural disasters are eligible.[2]
Trade Adjustment Act, amended by the Omnibus Trade and Competitiveness Act of 1988	A group of three or more people who have lost their jobs or are threatened to lose their jobs as a result of their firm being adversely affected by foreign imports. The firm's sales or production must have decreased, and their products must be in direct competition with imports.[3]
Economic Adjustment and Conversion— Personnel and Community Assistance (1992)	Workers and communities who experience job loss and economic distress as a result of defense cuts.
Economic Adjustment and Conversion— TRP (1992)	For TRP, firms and educational institutions compete for grants and must demonstrate how they can assist defense dependent firms diversify into commercial markets and create jobs for displaced workers.[4]
Adjustment Assistance to Workers Dislocated by NAFTA (1993)	A group of three or more workers who have lost their jobs or are threatened by job loss, and either: their firm's sales or production has decreased because their products are in direct competition with products produced in Canada or Mexico, or they have shifted production to Mexico or Canada.[5]

[1] CRS Issue Brief, *Unemployment Compensation: Proposals for Reform,* February 1, 1994.
[2] CRS Report for Congress, *Training for Dislocated Workers,* May 10, 1993.
[3] CRS Report, *Trade Adjustment Assistance: The Program for Workers,* September 22, 1993.
[4] CRS Report, *Adjustment Assistance to Workers Dislocated by NAFTA,* January 15, 1994.
[5] CRS Report for Congress, *Defense Conversion: Adjustment Assistance,* April 8, 1993.

does one determine whether or not someone is likely to return to a job or occupation? For example, a secretary who has been laid off from a large pharmaceutical firm may be ruled ineligible for retraining because secretarial jobs are still available. A telephone operator laid off from a telecommunications firm would quickly get retraining, but the secretary may need retraining to upgrade his or her skills just as much as the telephone operator.

The criteria identify some workers as eligible, but ignore others. For instance, a former Philadelphia Naval Yard employee may obtain assistance from UI and EAC, but the restaurant worker who served lunch to the Yard's employees only collects UI. Laid-off IBM employees in New York's mid-Hudson Valley get EDWAA placement, training assistance, *and* UI benefits. Laid-off workers in firms that supplied IBM's mainframe computer manufacturing plant may receive UI benefits, but not retraining aid.

Federal statutes give priority to the reason for dislocation. Often ignored are many dislocated workers who do not fit under these categories. Trade- or defense-related layoffs are considered more important than layoffs happening for other reasons. A dislocated worker whose position is eliminated due to federal trade policies qualifies for UI and may be eligible for EDWAA and TAA. Someone at AT&T who loses a job due to technological changes or even global competition may only be eligible for UI benefits.

By making some special industries and companies eligible for additional assistance, federal programs provide comprehensive services for some people and leave others to fend for themselves with only the help of an outdated unemployment system, unchanged since 1935. Moreover, the low level of available funds, combined with strict eligibility rules, means than many displaced workers receive no benefits whatsoever: unemployment insurance covers less than half of unemployed workers, and EDWAA serves less than 10 percent of *eligible* dislocated workers.[17]

WHAT SERVICES ARE PROVIDED?

Programs for the long-term unemployed have been pulled together in a piecemeal fashion by Congress over the last two decades, with each successive law adding new services. What has not occurred, however, is a reevaluation of the total system. Each new program makes incremental improvements, but the existing schemes are not updated to reflect changes in the economy or in the nature of unemployment.

The multiple employment and training programs are difficult for individuals to understand and access. Sue C. McAlister, an unemployed worker, complained of her frustration in getting into a retraining program before her unemployment benefits ran out: "If anybody thinks it's easy, they're crazy. You really have to be intelligent just to know what's happening."[18] Another unemployed worker pointed out that his unemployment insurance benefits were eliminated when he revealed to the state labor department that he was working part-time to put himself through a computer training program. "If they had told me there would be problems, I would not have enrolled," said Donald Ellis. What is particularly annoying to Mr. Ellis is that there are students enrolled in the same course who are collecting jobless benefits.[19]

The complex array of programs funded by the federal government frustrates displaced workers and employers. Program administration is diffused across several agencies; comprehensive services are available to some unemployed workers, but not others; duplication leads to higher administrative costs. For the unemployed, there are "no clear entry points and no clear path from one program to another," according to the General Accounting Office.[20] Intake and assessment may take weeks, if a person locates a program that has available funds.

The array of services provided under the major federal unemployment programs varies from program to program (see Figure 4.4). EDWAA and EAC offer the most comprehensive assistance. Under EDWAA, state-based "rapid-response teams" make immediate contact with employees affected by ongoing or projected layoffs. The newly unemployed are given information about emergency assistance and existing programs. The services provided to laid-off workers may consist of help in developing individual readjustment plans, job and career counseling, testing and assessment to determine occupational skills, and job search and placement assistance. Individuals may also obtain basic and remedial education and/or occupational retraining in the classroom or on the job. EDWAA also assists people looking for jobs in other states and helps them relocate if they find one. Support services include

FIGURE 4.4
Services Provided by Major Federal Programs

PROGRAM	SERVICES
Unemployment Insurance established by the Social Security Act of 1935	Intended as a temporary stopgap measure, the UI system provides weekly *cash transfers* to displaced workers for up to twenty-six weeks.[1]
Job Training Partnership Act amended, Title III, Economic and Worker Adjustment Assistance Act of 1988	*Cash transfers* for up to twenty-six weeks; other services provided through state PICs include: basic worker adjustment services, basic education training, classroom occupation training, and on the job training (OJT).[2]
Trade Adjustment Act, amended by the Omnibus Trade and Competitiveness Act of 1988	*Cash transfers* for up to fifty-two weeks for claimants who are enrolled in a TAA-approved training program. Other services include: basic worker adjustment services, basic education training, classroom occupational training, and relocation assistance up to $800.[3]
Economic Adjustment and Conversion— Personnel and Community Assistance (1992)	Aid to displaced workers include: *cash transfers*, basic worker adjustment services, and basic educational training under EDWAA; housing assistance (HUD); aid to communities and economic assistance (EAC/EDA).[4]
Economic Adjustment and Conversion— TRP	Aid to businesses includes: direct loans, marketing and management training, and technology deployment and development services through TRP.[5]
Adjustment Assistance to Workers Dislocated by NAFTA (1993)	*Cash transfers (TRAs)* are available to eligible workers for up to fifty-two weeks; other services include: basic worker adjustment services, basic education training, classroom occupational training, and OJT; and relocation assistance up to $800.[6]

[1] CRS Issue Brief, *Unemployment Compensation: Proposals for Reform*, February 1, 1994.
[2] CRS Report for Congress, *Training for Dislocated Workers*, May 10, 1993.
[3] CRS Report, *Trade Adjustment Assistance: The Program for Workers*, September 22, 1993.
[4] U.S. General Accounting Office, *Military Downsizing*, January 1994.
[5] Ibid.
[6] CRS Reprot, *Adjustment Assistance to Workers Dislocated by NAFTA*, January 15, 1994.

child care and transportation, pre-layoff assistance, and early intervention programs in cooperation with employers or labor groups.

Eligible workers can begin receiving all services, except relocation and support services, as soon as a public announcement of
a large-scale layoff is made. At that time, a labor-management
committee is established and charged with the task of developing
strategies that address the employment and training needs of affected workers. EDWAA-funded administrators also work with economic development agencies to prevent or reduce layoffs,
disseminate information on services for dislocated workers, and
assist communities in developing a response to dislocations.

While the training components of TAA and AANAFTA are
similar to those of EDWAA, the administrators responsible for
these programs follow a different path to obtain federal funds. The
process begins once a petition for TAA eligibility is filed with the
U.S. Department of Labor by an affected group of workers or
union. Eighty percent of the claims are decided within sixty days.
Once TAA requirements are met, workers are entitled to a weekly
cash sum equal to their most recent UI check for up to a year.
Other services for TAA-certified workers involved in training
include job search and placement, vocational testing, remedial education and referrals for training benefits, and relocation allowances
(up to $800).

Under EAC, communities and firms have a great deal of discretion in how the funds are utilized. Defense conversion monies
may be concentrated on communities, businesses, individuals, or
some combination of the three. Accordingly, the programs vary
widely in different jurisdictions.

PROGRAM IMPLEMENTATION

It is not surprising that individuals have trouble using the
employment and training system, because administrative responsibility is spread across federal, state, and local entities. Locally
based Private Industry Councils (PICs) under the Job Training
Partnership Act play an important role, as do thousands of private nonprofit and private for-profit training institutions, such as
community colleges and proprietary schools. At the federal level,

the U.S. Department of Labor oversees the implementation of the UI, TAA, EDWAA, AANAFTA, and the defense conversion programs. State-level responsibility is handled primarily by state labor departments (a summary of governance arrangements under the five principal programs is provided in Figure 4.5, page 146).

Unfortunately, the process of program implementation is not as neat and simple as this broad overview implies. For example, the Department of Labor allocates unemployment insurance to each of the fifty states and the District of Columbia based upon federal law. Each state is responsible for the administration and distribution of the weekly checks. States have different eligibility requirements and processes for helping jobless workers. Some states aggressively channel individuals into retraining programs; others confine themselves to handing out checks to the eligible unemployed.

The implementation of the Trade Adjustment Assistance Act is handled by the U.S. Department of Labor's Employment and Training Administration (ETA). The ETA processes the petitions of employee groups and unions for TAA funds, yet benefit distribution and training are administered by the state labor departments. And, firms adversely affected by import competition receive help from the U.S. Department of Commerce.[21]

EDWAA is administrated by the U.S. Department of Labor in conjunction with state labor departments and local PICs. EDWAA utilizes local officials and business leaders serving on PICs to develop strategies for the long-term unemployed. PIC members often have a better understanding of the needs of specific industries and workers than administrators based in state capitals. Eighty percent of the EDWAA funds go directly to local service delivery areas earmarked for the long-term unemployed, although states may hold back up to 20 percent for special projects, such as large-scale layoffs or disaster relief. The U.S. Department of Labor directly handles the remaining funds, with 15 percent distributed through discretionary grants and 5 percent used for technical assistance to the states.[22]

AANAFTA's entitlement component is incorporated into the TAA program; the discretionary component is part of JTPA. Both are administered by the U.S. Department of Labor. And although the Defense Conversion and Reinvestment program is thus primarily

FIGURE 4.5
Governance Structure of Major Federal Programs

PROGRAM	GOVERNANCE STRUCTURE
Unemployment Insurance established by the Social Security Act of 1935	Federal law provides guidelines with respect to eligibility, financing, and benefits. DoL allocates grants. Program is administered by each state.[1]
Job Training Partnership Act amended, Title III, Economic and Worker Adjustment Assistance Act of 1988	State government/governor has primary responsibility—coordinates and monitors state and local programs, determines SDAs, and appoints SJTCC. PICs appointed by local elected officials to provide planning and oversight of service delivery to consumers.[2]
Trade Adjustment Act, amended by the Omnibus Trade and Competitiveness Act of 1988	Administered by the Employment and Training Administration of the State DoL through SESAs. Training services provided through JTPA, which is overseen by federal, state, and local levels of government.[3]
Economic Adjustment and Conversion—Personnel and Community Assistance and TRP	EAC and DTCC agencies are responsible for assuring prompt notification to state/local bodies regarding eligibility for economic adjustment assistance resulting from cuts, realignment, and terminated contracts. Community groups and local governments and firms administer TRP/EAC/SBA and DTCC agency funds. Worker training programs are administered through DoL.[4]
Adjustment Assistance to Workers Dislocated by NAFTA (1993)	Governor determines preliminary eligibility and ensures rapid response and basic services to eligible groups of workers. Secretary of State and DoL determine final eligibility for worker assistance, which is administered by SESAs.[5]

[1] CRS Issue Brief, *Unemployment Compensation: Proposals for Reform,* February 1, 1994.
[2] CRS Report for Congress, *Training for Dislocated Workers,* May 10, 1993.
[3] CRS Report, *Trade Adjustment Assistance: The Program for Workers,* September 22, 1993.
[4] CRS Report for Congress, *Defense Conversion: Adjustment Assistance,* April 8, 1993.
[5] CRS Report, *Adjustment Assistance to Workers Dislocated by NAFTA,* January 15, 1994.

the responsibility of the U.S. Labor Department, it is overseen by an Economic Adjustment Committee, which is part of the Defense Department.

Governors have significant authority over the implementation of all the federal employment programs. While states have little flexibility in the application of eligibility rules and benefit levels, they can mold federal programs to their specific needs. Moreover, states have the authority to establish administrative structures to facilitate effective implementation. Thus, for example, several states have created human resource investment councils to provide meaningful oversight and coordination of all programs for the unemployed.

ARE THE PROGRAMS HELPING?[23]

UNEMPLOYMENT INSURANCE

During recessions when unemployment rises, government programs aimed at the unemployed logically are more heavily used. Before the latest recession, the overall rate of unemployment in the U.S. was 5.2 percent. It peaked in June 1992 at 7.6 percent and averaged 7.3 percent for the year.[24] Despite strong improvements in the economy, including the creation of over eight million jobs, the unemployment rate was still above 5.6 percent for 1995.[25] Following the trends in unemployment, spending for unemployment insurance rose dramatically during the recent recession. Moreover, the average UI weekly check increased over 30 percent, from $123 in 1984 to $182 in 1994.[26]

In gauging whether UI is effective, it might be more illuminating to examine the ratio of eligible workers to the number of workers actually served. Here, the record is less encouraging. The percentage of unemployed Americans covered by UI has been declining since the mid-1970s (see Table 4.2, page 148). About half of the unemployed in the U.S. were eligible for UI in the early 1970s. This proportion fell to one-third in the late 1980s. In 1992, at the height of the recession, 9.4 million people were jobless. However, unemployment insurance was only available to 3.4 million people, or 36 percent of the unemployed.[27] If the percentage of unemployed workers receiving unemployment insurance during the 1990–91 recession matched that during 1980, over 250,000

TABLE 4.2
Unemployment Insurance Program Coverage, Selected Years

Year	Total Unemployed	Unemployment Insurance Program	
		Number of People Insured	Percent of Total Unemployment
1974	5,156,000	2,558,000	49.6
1979	6,137,000	2,592,000	42.2
1984	8,539,000	2,560,000	29.9
1989	6,528,000	2,205,000	33.7
1990	6,874,000	2,575,000	37.4
1991	8,426,000	3,406,000	40.6
1992	9,384,000	3,348,000	35.6
1993	8,734,000	2,845,000	32.5
1994	7,996,000	2,746,000	34.3

Source: U.S. Council of Economic Advisers, Economic Report of the President, 1995 (Washington, D.C.: Government Printing Office, 1995), pp. 322–23.

fewer people would have fallen into poverty, according to the General Accounting Office.[28]

A combination of factors explains why UI coverage rates have dwindled in recent years.[29] For example, changes in the characteristics of the unemployed population have had an impact. Since UI benefits are paid to workers laid off from jobs that meet certain monetary and nonmonetary standards, the changing demographic composition of the workforce has caused a reduction in the number of unemployed covered under UI.

The decline of manufacturing employment and the rise of the service sector has also accounted for some of the reduction in coverage under UI. Most jobs in manufacturing, mining, and construction are included in the UI system, while many jobs in the service sector, such as restaurant workers, were not incorporated under UI until recently. But even if a good portion of service-sector workers are now in the system, the short-term nature of many of such jobs means that coverage will be less under the current rules, which pay greater benefits to those who were employed for longer periods. The extent to which these influences affect the coverage rate is difficult to measure; however, the Department of Labor believes they are significant.[30]

In the late 1970s and 1980s, the federal government implemented several policy changes that reduced UI coverage for the unemployed by altering the incentives for individuals to collect UI. Among the more important changes were the taxation of UI benefits, the classification of pensions under the Old Age Survivors and Disability Insurance (OASDI) program, revisions to the extended benefits programs, and alterations in the UI trust fund provisions.

In each case, the modifications created disincentives for sizable populations to participate in the UI system. The taxation of benefits reduced the wage replacement rate for recipients by as much as 25 to 30 percent. Thus, low-wage recipients had an incentive not to participate. When states deducted OASDI benefits, beginning in 1980, it was more difficult for older workers to collect benefits. In 1981, the eligibility requirements for TAA were severely tightened, weekly benefit amounts were reduced, and a cap was placed on the combined duration under UI and TAA. While the impact on TAA was significant, the effect on claims under UI was small.[31]

The federal government pressured states to enhance the solvency of the UI trust funds in the 1980s. New provisions deferred interest charges and future increases in the Federal Unemployment Tax Act (FUTA) taxes for states that reduced benefit payments and raised UI taxes.

Responding to the federal government's incentives, states adopted several changes that lowered the UI coverage rate. Some states increased the number of weeks one had to work before becoming eligible for UI. Other states implemented tougher definitions of "voluntary leaving" and "misconduct on the job as grounds for dismissal," thus eroding the coverage rate by altering operating definitions. Other states cut weekly benefit checks and thus reduced the incentive for unemployed individuals to apply for UI. Many states created tougher continuing eligibility requirements and tougher disqualification penalties.[32]

ECONOMIC DISLOCATION AND WORKER ADJUSTMENT ASSISTANCE ACT

Since the mid-1980s, the U.S. Department of Labor has collected information on the employment and earnings history of EDWAA participants for the first thirteen weeks after their completion of the program.[33] EDWAA served 312,000 people in program year 1992, which ran through June 30, 1993.

Sixty-nine percent of those who completed the program found a job for at least twenty hours per week. Sixty-four percent of those received some kind of retraining assistance, but only 28 percent were involved in retraining that lasted six months or more. Another 36 percent received only basic readjustment services, such as job search assistance and career counseling. Less than 10 percent received needs-based payments from EDWAA. The cost per participant averaged $1,460; the cost per participant who entered employment (those who got jobs) averaged $4,300.

EDWAA covers a diverse population with varying skills and work histories. In aggregate terms, just over half of the participants are men. More than two out of three are of prime working age (thirty to fifty-four years old). More than three in five have no more than a high school degree and only 13 percent graduated from college. About a fourth are members of minority groups.

There are many examples of successful EDWAA programs. For example, after Pan Am laid off several thousand employees, the federal government established a career center for former airline workers at Kennedy Airport. Under a $6 million grant, 2,323 of Pan Am's 2,500 displaced workers participated in the Career Connections program. Seventy-three percent of the participants got jobs. While Career Connections offered services ranging from counseling to copying services, the component cited by workers as the most helpful was the supportive environment created by the program.[34]

Another good example comes from the timber industry in Oregon. Nine out of ten unemployed millworkers and loggers who entered retraining programs at Lane Community College in Springfield, Oregon have obtained jobs. The average wages of the retrained workers is $9.00 per hour or about $1.00 per hour less than the average timber industry wage. Logging industry workers have been retrained as mechanics, cabinetmakers, and nurses.[35]

Unfortunately, the federal government has not made available detailed analysis of outcome data regarding those who completed the EDWAA program. For example, the U.S. Department of Labor has not released information comparing the participants' work experiences after completing the program with their personal characteristics, educational backgrounds, preprogram wages, or program activities. In order to further understand the impact of EDWAA, the Eagleton Institute analyzed surveys from over 45,000

EDWAA participants in six states over several years.[36] As with any secondary analysis, these data have limitations, but they offer one of the most comprehensive reviews available of EDWAA program outcomes.[37]

An important indicator of the success of training programs is how the wages earned by EDWAA participants compare with wages earned by other workers in a given state—the state's mean wage. In the Eagleton study, we found that 69 percent earned *less* than the state mean. These findings give some indication that EDWAA participants are not initially achieving average incomes after they complete the program.

The analysis of six states revealed that the participant's education level generally does not influence whether or not they hold a job thirteen weeks after the completion of the EDWAA program, nor whether that job is part-time or full-time.[38] The age of the participant is an important factor, however. Those over forty-four years of age are less likely to have jobs than their younger counterparts. Moreover, the youngest and oldest age groups are more likely to be working part-time rather than full-time.

The gender of the participant has little influence on rates of employment after EDWAA. In the six states, 68 percent of both men *and* women were working thirteen weeks after the completion of the program. Mirroring the rest of the labor force, postprogram wages were lower for women than men. Sixty-one percent of the men and 80 percent of the women earn less than the state average wage. Among employed participants, 72 percent of men and 58 percent of woman work full time.

There are only marginal differences among ethnic groups in the six-state study of EDWAA participants. Thirteen weeks after the program, 68 percent of whites are employed, but 67 percent of blacks, 64 percent of Hispanics, and 63 percent of Asians obtained jobs. Again, there are only small differences among part-time and full-time employment percentages across ethnic groups. Significant difference in earnings exist for ethnic groups, however. In the six-state study, 67 percent of whites earn below the state mean, while 89 percent of blacks, 81 percent of Hispanics, and 67 percent of Asians earn less than the mean.

Finally, we compared the postprogram experience of individuals according to the types of services given to them through

EDWAA. A majority of program participants, 55 percent, received basic readjustment services, such as job search assistance, résumé writing, and occupational assessment. Twenty-nine percent took occupational training courses, and only 3 percent were engaged in on-the-job training. After thirteen weeks, 68 percent of the program completers who received basic readjustment services found full-time employment, and 72 percent of the participants who were enrolled in occupational training courses were employed. In contrast, participants enrolled in on-the-job training fared much better: after thirteen weeks, 87 percent were employed.

On-the-job training participants also were more likely to get full-time jobs than those who received other EDWAA services. In the six states, 76 percent of on-the-job training participants were employed full-time, while 64 percent of those who had been in occupational training got full-time jobs.

TRADE ADJUSTMENT ASSISTANCE ACT

Under the Trade Adjustment Assistance Act, individuals must petition the Department of Labor to determine whether or not they are eligible for assistance. No doubt, there are American citizens who are eligible for TAA, but do not get help because they either are unaware of the program or do not wish to apply. There is no way to accurately estimate the size of this population because the Department of Labor only makes eligibility judgments based upon the applications it receives. But, detailed records are kept on the number of workers petitioning and accepted into the TAA program. Throughout the life of the program, the Department of Labor has approved about half of the applications for aid. Recently the approval rate has increased. In 1993 it was 44 percent, up from 36 percent in 1991.

Those who participate in the TAA program share many characteristics with displaced workers who participated in EDWAA.[39] They are unemployed for long periods of time prior to enrollment and have lost their jobs permanently. TAA participants are different in other respects, however. While displaced workers from the textile, rubber, and steel industries account for one-third of the total from the manufacturing sector, 85 percent of TAA participants come from these industries. Due to their concentration in unionized manufacturing firms, the prelayoff wages of TAA recipients are much higher than the average prelayoff wage for other displaced workers.

After the 1988 amendments to TAA, which placed priority on training, approximately one-half of enrollees received some form of training. Those enrolled in training tended to be younger and have more formal education than those who only received basic readjustment services. Most of those who received training felt it helped them get a job. The training requirement under TAA contributed to shortening the jobless period of participants and led to increases in earnings due to the more rapid reemployment.

TAA enrolls people who are likely to have a particularly difficult time finding reemployment. The average TAA participant receives over $10,000 worth of government benefits, including a combination of extended unemployment insurance benefits, job search allowances, and retraining services. TAA participants were less likely to have a job three years after their initial layoff than other displaced workers and experienced significant earnings losses—nearly $50,000 per worker. Three years after their layoff, more than three-quarters of those who found work earned less in their new jobs than they had earned previously.

Critics of the TAA program say that its mediocre performance record is due to poor program administration rather than to inherent flaws in program design.[40] TAA benefits are not equally accessible to all eligible workers because of the confusing and protracted certification process. Therefore, it takes too long for eligible people to get enrolled in the program. There is no careful targeting of appropriate services to insure that those who really need job search assistance or retraining get it. TAA program administrators in the state employment service offices do not provide adequate counseling and job search assistance to program participants before or after they participate in training programs. Like many programs, TAA is also assailed because its performance is not carefully monitored by the U.S. Department of Labor.

ADJUSTMENT ASSISTANCE TO WORKERS DISLOCATED BY THE NORTH AMERICAN FREE TRADE AGREEMENT

Although the program has only been in operation for nine months, preliminary data suggest that very few people are making claims under AANAFTA. Critics predicted that hundreds of thousands of workers would lose jobs due to NAFTA in its first year. Yet, the U.S. Department of Labor reports that only 10,345 people received special NAFTA benefits. Labor union officials and other critics contend that the low utilization of AANAFTA is due to ignorance of the program.

Insofar as NAFTA "victims" can be identified, they have been primarily unskilled workers engaged in manufacturing or assembly operations—furniture workers in Vancouver, Washington; stove manufacturers in Athens, Tennessee; and soap makers in Quincy, Massachusetts. A few days after NAFTA went into effect, for example, over 135 workers at a Nintendo assembly plant in Redmond, Washington, were laid off, their work transferred to a plant in Mexico.[41]

SUMMARY

Current U.S. unemployment policy is not a comprehensive strategy for addressing the problems of dislocated workers and the long-term unemployed. The U.S. economy has changed dramatically over the last ten to fifteen years, but federal policy has not kept pace with these changes. Federal lawmakers added several small-scale programs to combat new problems, but failed to reevaluate and reform existing ones. The result is a confusing mix of goals and delivery mechanisms that are difficult for unemployed individuals and companies to understand and use.

TAA, AANAFTA, and EAC assist industries and their dislocated workers in making the transition to new commercial markets. They are also designed to help create new markets and expand those that already exist. These industry- and occupation-specific programs help some individuals and companies in their transition to new jobs. However, if a single dislocated worker program existed at the federal level, then EAC, AANAFTA and TAA would be unnecessary.

Passive, cash transfer programs continue to dominate federal policy for several reasons. Unemployment insurance has a strong constituency that soundly opposes efforts to change its basic structure. UI is viewed by many as a political entitlement. Suggestions that recipients should engage in job search activities or enter retraining programs are assailed by unions as taking away a hard-won entitlement of working Americans.

UI is easier to administer than more complicated interventions, like retraining or technology reinvestment programs. As an entitlement program with significant political support, UI escapes careful scrutiny. Standards for assessing UI are simple: "Is the money distributed to the right people in a timely manner?" In contrast, evaluating the success of training programs is harder because the goals are more ambitious. Training programs are supposed to help people get new jobs with earnings roughly equivalent to the trainee's previous employment.

Private-sector firms support current programs and policies regarding the unemployed because they retain flexibility in managing their workforces. UI is supported by taxes on the employer and, in a few states, on employees. UI taxes increase only modestly if a company routinely lays off employees. It is estimated that the UI cost to a typical employer for laying off a worker is about three weeks' wages in the form of increased UI tax liability[42]

The increases in UI premiums are viewed by most companies as an acceptable cost for dropping employees. Bearing this cost ensures that they can shave overhead during slow business cycles, and the UI cash transfer system ensures that most of their workforce will stay in the area while they seek new work. Thus, UI cash transfers help increase the likelihood that workers will be *available* when they are needed again.

Underlying current federal unemployment programs is the assumption that people acquire sufficient skills for a working lifetime by the time they complete high school or college. Therefore, the government relies on temporary income support as its response to joblessness rather than large-scale retraining programs.

A quite different view holds that the needs of the labor market are changing rapidly and that firms need a workforce with improving skills. The unemployed should improve their skills in order to get jobs and the economy needs a skilled workforce in order to create growth and opportunity. Proponents of this view argue that society's obligation does not end once formal education has been completed. This approach, which is reflected in some small but important federal programs, concludes that government has an important, legitimate role in providing training. Thus far, however, the federal government has not applied this theory to its main public employment and training programs.

5

STATES TO THE RESCUE?

The federal government spends billions of dollars a year on worker adjustment assistance in the form of unemployment insurance (UI) and retraining. These programs are offered to individuals who are already unemployed, or are about to lose their jobs, to help them regain a foothold on the economic ladder. Are the states trying different strategies? The answer is both yes and no.

Most states merely extend or embellish federal programs to further cushion the blow of unemployment. A small but growing number of states are meeting the challenge of economic transition with strategies that have not received much support at the federal level. These state worker-adjustment programs are modest in budgetary resources, but they are significant because state intervention often happens *before* layoffs occur, reflecting the traditional state concern over economic development. An even smaller number of states have enacted laws that regulate private sector behavior with regard to how layoffs are conducted and the private sector's responsibility to workers.

This chapter summarizes the results of a comprehensive survey of state worker-adjustment programs and examines several states with mature programs. The workforce adjustment strategies discussed here may be distinguished from traditional economic development programs that provide general assistance to firms for equipment, training, and buildings because workforce strategies target unemployed individuals or those at risk of unemployment.

AN OVERVIEW OF STATE WORKFORCE
ADJUSTMENT STRATEGIES

States implement most federal unemployment programs including unemployment insurance, labor exchange services, the Trade Adjustment Assistance Act (TAA), and the bulk of the Economic Dislocation and Worker Adjustment Assistance Act (EDWAA). Thirty-three states do nothing more than carry out their federally prescribed responsibilities. But seventeen other states have created their own approaches (see Figure 5.1, pages 159–61). In fiscal year 1994, these seventeen states spent a total of approximately $380 million on workforce adjustment programs. Spending has increased substantially in the past three years.[1] The annual state commitment to worker adjustment programs varies from $185,000 in North Dakota to the nearly $150 million spent by California's Employment and Training program. Substantial funding is also available in New Jersey, Massachusetts, Minnesota, and Washington.

Although state spending is tiny relative to the more than $30 billion spent on federal programs for the unemployed, it is more appropriate to compare the states' $380 million commitment with the $1.4 billion in federal spending on EDWAA. The state programs generally do not furnish income replacement, but rather, like EDWAA, provide job search assistance and training for the long-term unemployed. For example, New Jersey's $50 million Workforce Development Partnership Program funds more workforce adjustment assistance than the state's share of federal EDWAA and TAA combined, even after taking into account the huge increases made in EDWAA in the past three years.

State programs are financed through a variety of mechanisms. While general revenues are the primary sources of funding for state programs, California, New Jersey, Massachusetts, Minnesota, and Washington collect funds by adding incremental charges to the unemployment insurance tax; Oregon uses money generated by the state lottery; Iowa generates money from withholding taxes from the creation of new jobs and increased property taxes generated through corporate investment in plant and equipment. Indiana and Wisconsin support programs with general funds.

The missions of state-funded assistance programs are diverse. Some follow the federal approach of cash transfer payments and

FIGURE 5.1
State Programs for Unemployed Workers

STATE	PROGRAM	EXPENDITURES	PERIOD	PROGRAM DESCRIPTION	TARGET GROUP
Alaska	State Training and Employment Program	$2,600,000	Annually	The purpose of this program is to reduce claims against Unemployment Insurance, foster new jobs, and increase training opportunities for dislocated workers.	The unemployed
California	Employment Training Panel (ETP)	$148,800,000	1992-93	The ETP contracts private sector providers to assist businesses in obtaining skilled workers to stay competitive, productive, and profitable and training for new and existing employees.	Businesses, current employees, and dislocated workers
Delaware		$825,000	Annually	Counseling, training, and placement for dislocated workers	Dislocated workers
Indiana	Public Law 38	$3,500,000	Annually	Counseling, training, and placement for dislocated workers	Dislocated workers
Iowa	New Jobs Training Program and the Jobs Training Program	$3,069,300	Annually	Iowa's Division of Work Force Development provides loans or grants to train existing employees for companies that are retooling or new employees for new or expanding firms.	Businesses and their current employees
Maine		$1,300,000	Annually	Readjustment and retraining assistance to the unemployed.	The unemployed
Massachusetts	Training Opportunities Program	$50,000,000	Annually	Allows eligible unemployment insurance claimants to collect unemployment benefits while attending approved short-term intensive training.	Unemployment insurance claimants

Continued

FIGURE 5.1
State Programs for Unemployed Workers (Continued)

STATE	PROGRAM	EXPENDITURES	PERIOD	PROGRAM DESCRIPTION	TARGET GROUP
Minnesota	State Dislocated Workers Program	$21,500,000	1993–94	This state program was designed to supplement EDWAA. Provides training to workers displaced from firms with fifty or more employees.	Displaced workers
Montana		$500,000		Temporary supplement to EDWAA. Serves state workers who have been recently laid off.	Laid off state workers
New Jersey	Workforce Development Partnership Program	$50,000,000	Annually	Upgrades skills of existing workforce, provides training for the unemployed, strengthens linkages between the elements of New Jersey's worker readiness system.	Businesses, dislocated workers, and those at risk of dislocation
New Mexico	Industrial Development Training Fund	$6,000,000	1994	Classroom and on-the-job training for dislocated workers and those at risk of being laid off.	Dislocated workers and workers at risk of dislocation
North Carolina	Employment and Training Program	$2,400,000	Annually	Issues grants to local agencies for local employment and training programs. Programs upgrade basic skills, provide on-the-job training, work experience, adult basic education, counseling, screening for job placement, and other support services.	Dislocated workers
North Dakota	Workforce 2000	$185,000	1993	Retraining and skills upgrading for new technologies or work methods for dislocated workers and workers at risk of dislocation (employer contributions to this program for FY94 is $1.9 million).	Dislocated workers and those at risk of dislocation

State	Program	Expenditures	Period	Program Description	Target Group
Oregon	Dislocated Worker Program	$4,750,000	1993–95	Retraining, basic readjustment services and income maintenance to dislocated workers. Implemented jointly by the state's community college system, State Employment Division, and the Job Training Partnership Administration.	Dislocated workers
Pennsylvania		$3,500,000		General retraining and reemployment services for dislocated workers whose UI benefits have expired.	UI claimants whose benefits have expired
Washington	Workforce Employment and Training Act	$40,000,000	1993–94	Job training and employment in healthy industries, including funding of education degrees. Established pilot projects under a partnership with the State Board for Community & Technical Colleges. Emphasized outreach to employers and increased technology in transmission of information (unemployment claimant registration by phone, statewide job listings via computer, etc.)	Dislocated workers
Washington	Entrepreneurial Program	$304,000	1993–95	Classes in business planning, basic business accounting, entrepreneurial functions and ongoing support for dislocated wood products workers to start and maintain their own businesses.	Dislocated wood products workers
Wisconsin	Dislocated Worker Program	$500,000	Annually	Supplements EDWAA expenditures for training, retraining, and cash transfers.	Dislocated workers

Source: Derived from a survey of administrators conducted from March through May of 1994 by the Eagleton Institute of Politics, Rutgers University.

retraining. Programs in Minnesota, Massachusetts, and North Carolina, for example, emphasize the principle that government's role is to respond after layoffs occur. Others states have more ambitious goals, retraining workers who are at risk of losing their jobs. California, Iowa, Indiana, New Mexico, and New Jersey work in partnership with private sector firms to help workers weather economic change. Clearly, there are overlapping missions. Many states dispense both prelayoff assistance and aid for the unemployed. Indiana's program focuses on dislocated workers, but it also tries to increase the competitiveness of its businesses and workforce in order to prevent future worker dislocations.

Helping Laid-off Workers

Many state-funded worker adjustment programs furnish additional cash assistance to jobless residents. Some extend unemployment benefits for several weeks or months. Supporters of these programs argue that such aid is necessary because growing numbers of displaced workers are exhausting federal benefits before they can find another job.[2] But, there are severe restrictions on what the states can do on their own. States that charge employers high payroll taxes may put themselves at a disadvantage in interstate competition for economic development.

States began legislating UI benefit extensions in the late 1950s. By 1970, ten states had extended provisions for the unemployed who had exhausted their federal assistance. In 1990, federal government adopted the Extended Unemployment Compensation Act, which provided for full federal funding of extended benefits programs when authorized by Congress. Since then, states have played a smaller role in lengthening benefit periods. Nevertheless, during the last recession a few states—California, Connecticut, New Jersey, and Washington—enacted extended benefits programs.

Four states—Massachusetts, New Jersey, Oregon, and Washington—extend UI benefits to individuals enrolled in training programs. For example, Massachusetts' Training Opportunities Program gives clients up to an additional eighteen weeks of unemployment benefits beyond the state's basic thirty-week benefit period. States' policymakers hope that additional assistance encourages people to acquire the extra training that might reduce the likelihood of future episodes on the unemployment rolls.

Other states, including Indiana, Minnesota, Montana, and Wisconsin, funnel state monies directly into the EDWAA delivery system. State strategies modeled after EDWAA provide identical services—retraining and payments to dislocated workers who have exhausted their unemployment insurance benefits. It is also not surprising that these states utilize the Job Training Partnership Act's delivery system—Service Delivery Areas and Private Industry Councils.

A few states offer EDWAA-like services, but target resources to different populations. For example, Washington created an Entrepreneurial Training Program, which targets, as a first priority, dislocated workers living or working in communities that were dependent on the wood products industry. Washington's program assists dislocated workers who wish to start their own businesses. It features instruction in the skills needed to function successfully as a business owner/manager, including business plan development, financial and loan packaging, accounting and taxes, and wholesale and retail sales. The program also includes continuing assistance to those who start their own enterprise.

In establishing state workforce adjustment strategies, some states require that workers be permanently separated from the employer for whom they worked. Others target workers displaced by structural shifts in particular industries. For example, Indiana's job training program requires that individuals must have been dislocated within five years of enrollment and must not have had intervening employment providing 80 percent or more of previous wages and benefits.[3] None of the state programs imposed any income test on participants, however.

Massachusetts' eligibility criterion is unemployment, but workers must demonstrate that they have little chance of obtaining employment without training. Massachusetts' Training Opportunities Program aided approximately 16,000 people in the past two years, out of 300,000 unemployed state residents. Minnesota, Oregon, Washington, and Wisconsin utilize EDWAA criteria for accepting clients. While they accept dislocated workers, intake standards are very flexible because any unemployed person may receive services.

In Washington's Workforce Employment and Training Act, also known as the "1988 program," participants may enroll in college for up to two years to complete associates degrees.[4] A trust fund was established for the program by diverting a portion of the payroll tax paid by businesses for unemployment insurance, but employer taxes were not increased. Approximately $44 million will be generated for the fund during the 1993–95 period. The program allocates $35 million to create over 5,000 new student positions at the state's thirty-two community colleges. Each enrollment slot is funded at $3,200. Students are expected to contribute approximately $1,000 of their own money toward their education.

The Washington program also addresses the situation in which unemployed workers are denied unemployment benefits if they are unavailable for full-time work, thus making it more difficult for them to engage in retraining. Under the program, unemployed workers enrolled in training programs approved by the state Department of Labor may continue to receive unemployment benefits.

Nearly 900 full-time student positions for 1993–94 were set aside for laid-off Boeing Aircraft workers from the Puget Sound area. Other large retraining programs were established by laid-off timber mill workers. Occupation-specific training is also provided by higher education institutions. For example, Spokane Community College is providing preapprenticeship lineman training for individuals who will enter $12 per hour jobs in utility districts, and Clover Park Community College is training specialists in environmental technology. Job-specific training may be carried out in coordination with private-sector employers.

Oregon's Choices and Options Program relies on its state college system to implement dislocated worker services. State and community colleges provide workshops on job training opportunities, resume writing, interviewing, and job search skills. Community colleges are often able to respond quickly to the training needs of firms. Businesses are increasingly seeking partnerships with higher education to help them cope with changing workforce needs. Oregon's Apprenticeship Program prepares laid-off workers for occupations in industries that state officials foresee as growth sectors. In 1993, the program assisted 500 unemployed individuals.

Helping Workers at Risk of Displacement

States use worker training programs to persuade companies to remain in their states and expand operations. Known as "customized training," these programs are also used as a lure for businesses considering relocation. For example, substantial training programs for new workers were tendered by South Carolina in its bid to convince BMW to locate its first U.S.-based manufacturing plant there.

Analytically, one would like to distinguish between training programs that are used as an incentive for economic growth versus programs designed to prevent economic decay and unemployment. As a practical matter, however, it is extremely difficult to make these distinctions. What we know is that state training programs are popular means of economic development, and customized training programs have mushroomed because of intense interstate competition, rather than in response to the needs of workers at risk of losing their jobs.

More interesting for this review, however, are retraining programs primarily used to retrain unemployed workers or to upgrade the skills of a company's existing workforce. A few states offer retraining programs that enable workers to upgrade their skills and keep up with the demands of technological change and economic competition. Such strategies move beyond the concept of healing the economically wounded. Instead, they are intended to avoid long-term unemployment by targeting individuals at risk of losing their jobs. For example, the Workers at Risk Program in Indiana's PL-38 Program hopes to avoid worker dislocations through training grants to employers. "At risk" businesses are determined through a set of indicators, including financial losses in three of the past eight quarters, an unfavorable debt-to-asset ratio, and significant layoffs over the past year. Over 1,600 individuals benefitted from this program in fiscal year 1992–93.

California's Employment and Training Panel

California's Employment and Training Panel (ETP) is the largest and oldest state-funded workforce adjustment program in the states. ETP is a cooperative business-labor program created by the California legislature in 1982. It was funded by a 0.1 percent payroll tax assessed on all employers with a positive reserve in their UI account. Initially, this new tax was offset by a cut in regular payroll taxes. Since then, the tax rate has been independently set and is therefore a straight tax for training and retraining. ETP assists businesses in obtaining skilled workers so that the firm remains competitive, productive, and profitable. ETP funds training for the unemployed receiving UI as well as those who have exhausted UI benefits. The largest component of ETP consists of programs for "potentially displaced workers who would otherwise become unemployment insurance claimants."

ETP's first priority is training for new hires or retraining for workers who have received notification of actual layoff. The program targets resources to individuals employed in small businesses, defined by statute as those with fewer than 250 employees.[5] In 1992–93, 60 percent of all the funds were committed to small businesses, whereas in 1990–91, it was only 26 percent.

ETP recipients are given at least 100 hours of classroom, laboratory, and/or structured on-site training through a network of public and private providers contracted by the state. ETP funds training conducted by the firm as well as by nonprofit organizations, local education agencies, and Private Industry Councils. Preference is given to proposals developed jointly by management and worker representatives.

In 1992–93, ETP trained workers at 2,785 firms. Fifty percent of contracts and funding were granted to manufacturing concerns during fiscal year 1992–93, whereas manufacturing comprises less than 6 percent of the California workforce. About 30 percent of the contracts were awarded to service-sector firms, which employ nearly half of the state's workers. Some examples of projects undertaken by ETP include retraining 500 current Aetna Life and Casualty employees in office automation, customer service, and statistical process controls; retraining 1,100 employees of the American Institute of Banking in sales techniques and management skills; and retraining 750 journey-level workers from the International Association of Machinists and various car dealerships in mechanical and body repair skills.

ETP has strict performance-based contracts with training institutions. Vendors are not paid until *after* a worker is retained on a job for which the training was provided for at least ninety days. Other notable features of ETP are its employer-driven quality, strong support and involvement of unions, and heavy reliance on private training providers.

New Jersey's Workforce Development Partnership Program

The Workforce Development Partnership Program (WDPP), started in 1992, is the only other state-funded workforce adjustment strategy that matches the commitment offered in California. The five-year, $250 million program consists of three elements: employer-based training for incumbent workers, vouchers for dislocated workers to obtain training, and extended benefits for the unemployed who are engaged in training.

WDPP awards training grants to employers seeking to create, retain, or upgrade jobs in demand occupations, with an emphasis on so-called high-wage, high-skill jobs.[6] Union concurrence is required for companies that have collective bargaining agreements. Over half of the participating firms involved to date are unionized. The firms must promise to hire or retain individuals who successfully complete training.

Firms have trained workers in a broad range of skills—from basic training for new hires to basic math and English and second language skills. But by far the most common activity—conducted by half the firms—has been to train workers in the use of modern manufacturing processes, such as "just-in-time" or demand-flow production systems. Basic skills training was the next most popular activity. Total quality management was offered by 35 percent of the firms.

Eight in ten of the grants were given to manufacturing firms in the first year. Half of the awards were made to small- and medium-sized firms, those with fewer than 250 employees. Recipient firms must provide at least 40 percent of the total program costs. In fact, employers claim to have contributed 70 percent of the cost of training, or $24 million, to match the $10 million awarded by the state in WDPP's first year. The most common employer contribution is "released time," that is, time for workers to attend training. In the first year of WDPP's operation the state awarded nearly half of the retraining funds, or nearly $5 million, to the General Motors' Linden Assembly plant. The balance of the grants to 42 firms averaged $130,000.

WDPP also offers individual training grants whereby unemployed workers are empowered to pursue training through a voucher system with approved vendors. WDPP stresses higher skilled training, although remedial education is made available to about 2 percent of participants. The program is directed at applicants with good work histories and demonstrated levels of achievement—individuals with strong prospects for success. It is not regarded as an "entitlement" for all displaced workers.

During the first year of operation, over 10,000 unemployed workers got vouchers worth a total of $30 million for training services, or an average grant of just under $3,000 per worker. Guidance in selecting occupational skills and training programs that would best meet individual needs was furnished by the state labor department. The most popular forms of training were clerical and sales (25 percent), professional technical and managerial (14 percent), and medicine and health care (14 percent). Training vendors consist primarily of proprietary schools and two-year colleges. Four-year colleges and vocational-technical schools also train individual grant recipients.

An important feature of WDPP is the provision of additional UI benefits for certain individuals enrolled in training. The idea was to encourage unemployed workers to take advantage of longer, in-depth training opportunities and thus prepare for high-skilled occupations in which labor shortages are expected to arise. Roughly one-third of the 10,000 people receiving WDPP training grants also received additional UI benefits worth an average of $3,800. Over half of the WDPP participants receiving additional benefits during training enrolled in programs that lasted six months or more.

Although commendable for the flexibility they provide, voucher programs place a burden on counselors and clients. Such systems are not successful unless complete and timely information regarding client needs and training facilities is available. Without this, client and counselor cannot make intelligent decisions. At this time, it is not possible to assess how well WDPP administrators are handling this task.

The Performance of State
Workforce Adjustment Programs

Employment rates, wages, and retention rates are most often used to evaluate the effectiveness of dislocated worker programs. Evaluating programs designed to prevent layoffs is even more difficult. Detailed information on the efficacy and efficiency of state-supported workforce adjustment strategies is lacking. Only a few states have comprehensive evaluation and monitoring systems. Without better evaluations it is impossible to determine whether or not these state-based workforce adjustment programs merit replication in other states or expansion through federal statutes. The information from California's ETP, which has the most complete track data on clientele, firms, and impacts, is encouraging. (Additional evidence about other states is summarized in Figure 5.2, page 170.)

ETP trained 13,532 individuals in fiscal year 1992–93. Of those, 12,381 (91 percent) were workers at risk of dislocation whose skills were then upgraded or who were retrained for new jobs in their firm. The rest of those served were new hires.[7]

ETP retrainees increased their earnings by $4,500—15 percent—in the year after training, and previously unemployed workers who completed training increased their earnings by $10,000—88 percent—a year after completing training, according to a study conducted by the California State University at Northridge. The California state study also found that these gains in income persisted two years after program completion. In the year following training, those who completed ETP were unemployed fewer weeks and received less in unemployment insurance than those who dropped out.[8] These findings may exaggerate the positive benefits, because there is no control group comparison. Nevertheless, the reported gains are significant indicators of positive performance because they reflect adjusted earnings beyond inflation.

One criticism leveled against workforce programs such as WDPP and ETP is that they subsidize the private sector by providing training that would otherwise be provided by the firms themselves.[9] As economists Paul Osterman and Rosemary Batt point out, "The risk is heightened by the very nature of employer-centered training. When a firm proposes a training program, it is

FIGURE 5.2
Outcomes of State-Funded Programs

STATE PROGRAM	PERFORMANCE MEASURES
California Employment Training Panel (ETP)	In fiscal year 1993, there were 13,532 individuals trained and employed; 2,785 businesses were served, 83 percent of which were small businesses. The program resulted in an 88 percent increase in average annual earnings for new hires and 15 percent for retrainees.
Indiana Public Law 38	In fiscal year 1993, there were 1,617 individuals trained.
Massachusetts Training Opportunities Program	In fiscal year 1993, there were 8,000 individuals trained; 84 percent found employment.
Minnesota State Dislocated Workers Program	Approximately 10,000–12,000 individuals receive training each year. The state responds to every plant closing of fifty or more employees—approximately 60–70 percent of the state's layoffs.
New Jersey Workforce Development Program	In fiscal year 1993 and fiscal year 1994, there were 10,169 individual training recipients. Those served received an average of $3,805 in additional Unemployment Insurance benefits, and $2,987 in training vouchers. Fifty-six grants have been issued to employers for customized training efforts.
Oregon Dislocated Worker Program	This program seeks to serve 6,300 dislocated workers each biennium. Approximately 80 percent of these workers have received some form of training or workshop.
Washington Workforce Employment and Training Act	This program began in the fall of 1993 with an enrollment of 1,164. The enrollment goal for 1993–94 was 3,500.
Entrepreneurial Program	This program served 243 individuals in the 1991–93 biennium; seventy-two individuals successfully completed the program and started their own businesses.
Wisconsin Dislocated Worker Program	This program seeks to serve 800–900 people each year. Actual data on clients served was unavailable.

Source: Derived from a survey of administrators conducted from March through May of 1994 by the Eagleton Institute of Politics, Rutgers University.

very difficult for the state agency to determine whether the effort will be a net addition to what the firms would have otherwise undertaken."[10]

The broad standards for participation in ETP and WDPP can invite abuse by private firms. Shrewd private-sector managers can transfer their retraining costs to the state's taxpayers by claiming financial hardship and threatening to close. This is especially true of large firms. It is for this reason, among others, that ETP and WDPP have focused the bulk of their resources on small- and medium-sized businesses.

State policymakers have also guarded against these tactics by requiring substantial contributions from firms by carefully screening business plans. Retraining projects are likely to have the greatest impact when they are integrated into the company's plans for improving competitiveness, when retraining is a critical factor in improving company performance, when retraining provides workers with *transferable* skills that are in demand in the labor market, and when businesses are unlikely to undertake retraining without outside intervention.[11]

Another concern raised about state-funded workforce adjustment strategies, such as ETP, is that they train workers who are most likely to succeed. ETP's payment scheme, which only reimburses training providers who successfully place individuals, encourages this behavior. The characteristics of individuals enrolled in the ETP tend to support this criticism. While 21 percent of the unemployed population in California have less than a high school education, this was true of only 4 percent of the enrollees in the ETP.[12] ETP has tried to deal with this issue by providing special funds for job-based literacy training and remedial education.

REGULATING LAYOFFS

Several states have imposed regulations governing how employers instigate layoffs and how they treat their former employees (see Figure 5.3, pages 172–75). Thirteen states enacted laws increasing the obligations of employers toward their workers. Such approaches may or may not discourage hiring. It is also unclear whether or not they discourage layoffs. In a climate of fierce interstate competition, policymakers are willing to gamble that these

FIGURE 5.3
State Legislation Covering Advance Notice, Severance, and Health Benefit Continuation

STATE	ADVANCE NOTICE	SEVERANCE	HEALTH BENEFITS
Connecticut			Covers employers of one hundred or more persons during the preceding twelve months. Requires employer to pay in full for the continuation of existing health insurance for 120 days.
Hawaii		Covers any employer of fifty or more employees during the preceding twelve-month period. Requires employer to pay a dislocated worker allowance. The allowance is a supplement to unemployment compensation and is equal to the difference between the claimant's unemployment weekly benefit amount and the claimant's old salary for a period of four weeks.	
Maine		Covers any employer who relocates or terminated a covered establishment (a facility with one-hundred or more employees during the preceding twelve months). Employees must have been in their positions for the preceding three years. The severance amount is equal to one week's pay for each year of employment.	

State	Advance Notice	Severance	Health Benefits
Maryland	Covers any employer that reduces the number of employees by 25 percent or fifteen employees, whichever is greater, over any three-month period. **Calls for the development of voluntary guidelines for employers regarding advanced notification and continuation of benefits.		**(See Advance Notice)
Massachusetts		If a company is purchased, the buyer must pay two weeks severance for each year of service to employees with three or more years of service. Law applies to closures within two years of the transfer of ownership of the company.	
Michigan	Encourages employers to give notice of plant closure whenever possible where twenty-five or more persons are employed.		
Nevada			Allows for thirty-six months minimum continuation of coverage for spouse and dependent of employee who is involuntarily terminated. Terminated worker eligible for eighteen months' continuation of coverage as under COBRA.

Continued

FIGURE 5.3
State Legislation Covering Advance Notice, Severance, and Health Benefit Continuation (Continued)

STATE	ADVANCE NOTICE	SEVERANCE	HEALTH BENEFITS
Oregon	Designates a state agency to receive notification of plant closings as required under federal WARN legislation.		
Pennsylvania		If a company is purchased, the buyer must pay one week severance for each year of service to employees with two or more years of service. Law applies to closures within two years of the transfer of ownership of the company.	
Rhode Island		If a company is purchased, the buyer must pay two week severance for each year of service to employees with three or more years of service. Law applies to closures within two years of the transfer of ownership of the company OR when a buyer increases ownership of voting securities from 5 to 50 percent.	

State	Advance Notice	Severance	Health Benefits
Tennessee	Covers any person, corporation, or other entity that employs at least fifty but no more than ninety-nine full-time employees permanently or indefinitely displaces fifty or more during any three-month period. Requires employer to notify employees and state.		
Washington			Insurance company must offer policy-holder option to convert to individual coverage if they become ineligible for coverage for any reason.
Wisconsin	Covers employers displacing twenty-five or more (or 25 percent, whichever is greater) employees and that employs fifty or more persons in the state. Requires sixty days' notice prior to plant closing or layoff.		

Source: Ronald Green, William Carmell, and Jerrold Goldberg. 1993 State by State Guide to Human Resources Law (New York: Panel Publications, 1992), pp. 120–25.

regulations will not be used as a club against them in negotiations with firms threatening to leave the state.

ADVANCE NOTICE

The federal Worker Adjustment Retraining and Notification Act (WARN) requires employers to provide up to sixty days advance notice to individuals who will be laid off, or to provide them with severance payments in lieu of notice. WARN's requirements do not apply to takeovers or other reorganizations of the firm and are frequently ignored by employers.

WARN does not prevent states from enacting their own laws governing business cutbacks, relocations, and sales. Hawaii, Maine, Maryland, Massachusetts, Michigan, Oregon, Tennessee, Washington, and Wisconsin have early notification requirements. It is not known whether they work more effectively than the federal statute.[13] State laws seek extended notice protection for employees in firms not covered by federal statute. None demand notification in excess of the federal minimum, however.[14] Moreover, the penalties for failing to comply are minimal in all states except Hawaii, where employees have the right to sue for damages and employers are subject to fines equal in value to three months' wages and benefits.[15]

SEVERANCE PAY

Hawaii, Maine, Massachusetts, Pennsylvania, and Rhode Island have adopted laws stipulating severance payments for laid-off workers. Firms with more than fifty employees that lay off workers in Hawaii because of a sale, transfer, merger, or other business takeover are required to pay severance. Known as a "dislocated worker allowance," the pay must equal the difference between the employee's salary and their unemployment insurance benefits for four weeks. Maine employers are required to pay each laid-off employee with three or more years of seniority one week's wages for each year of service.[16]

Pennsylvania, Rhode Island, and Massachusetts afford protection to employees affected by corporate takeovers or mergers. For example, if a company in Massachusetts is purchased, the buyer must pay two weeks severance for each year of service to laid-off employees with three or more years of service.[17]

EXTENDED HEALTH BENEFITS

Under the federal Consolidated Omnibus Budget Recon-
struction Act (COBRA), workers are given the opportunity to convert employers' group health insurance coverage to individual
coverage for period of eighteen months. Many states have adopted laws requiring insurance companies to extend additional group
health insurance benefits for individuals. New Hampshire employees may remain covered under the firm's group health coverage
for thirteen weeks prior to conversion to COBRA.

Only Connecticut and Nevada move substantially beyond
COBRA's requirements. Connecticut law requires employers that
are closing their businesses or relocating out of state, and who
employ 100 or more workers, to pay for 120 days of continued
group health insurance and allow employees to maintain such coverage for an additional thirty-nine weeks at their own expense.
Nevada allows for three years of minimum continuation for the
spouse and dependents of anyone who is involuntarily terminated.[18]

SUMMARY

Innovative strategies in the states reflect needs and characteristics of
different regions that are not satisfied by federal policy initiatives.
The development of state-funded workforce adjustment strategies is
a political reaction to the alarming increase in dislocated workers.
As the predicament deepened in the late 1980s, additional funding
was not forthcoming from the federal government. Many governors and legislators decided to enact state-specific economic dislocation programs. With state budgets strapped for cash and the
recent threefold increase in federal EDWAA funding under the
Clinton administration, Governors and state legislatures may try
to scale back their initiatives.

Workforce adjustment strategies are a natural outgrowth of
interstate competition for economic development. State policymakers
have begun to view workforce development as a potentially effective strategy for stimulating economic growth—either by attracting
new businesses or retaining old ones. Growing global competition
and increasing technology produced gaps between employer needs
and worker skills.

State-based policies also reflect the frustration of state officials with means-tested federal job training programs under the
principal Job Training Partnership Act program and federal welfare
reform. State policymakers have been interested in avoiding the
stigma associated with federal, income-targeted job training programs.[19] Moreover, no federal program funds have been available
to help fund training for incumbent workers.

States on the cutting edge of workforce development recognize
the opportunity this environment provides, not only to fill gaps in
workforce preparedness and employer demands, but also to step
out ahead of neighboring states, to keep and grow existing businesses and attract new businesses through competitive education
and training programs. Simultaneously, these states are addressing growing unemployment and the burden that displaced workers
put on social services.

Research on the impact of state-funded programs is encouraging, albeit quite limited. Retrainee wages increased substantially after training in California's ETP program. State programs have
also helped stimulate concern for creating high-performance workplaces. State-subsidized training is helping to prevent layoffs by
overcoming employer uncertainty over the introduction of new
technologies and work processes. Thus, according to a National
Commission for Employment Policy report, "state programs may
play a major catalytic role in encouraging businesses to use training as an agent of strategic change and establish permanent learning systems within companies."[20]

Despite state innovations, shortcomings persist. The change-
over from passive cash transfer programs to active human capital
investment strategies has been very limited. Further evolution is
hindered by federal regulations and by the lack of adequate funds
to meet the demand for services. Innovation has also bred duplication and confusion in service delivery, making program inventory
and review difficult. In the absence of more systematic evaluations
of state-funded workforce adjustment strategies, federal policy
makers may be reluctant to adopt many of the innovations under
way.

Notes

Chapter 1

1. An unemployed steel worker quoted in William Serrin, *Homestead: The Glory and Tragedy of an American Steel Town* (New York: Times Books, 1992), p. 387.

2. Kenneth Jost, "Downward Mobility," *CQ Researcher*, July 23, 1993, p. 627.

3. U.S. Council of Economic Advisers, *Economic Report of the President, 1994* (Washington, D.C.: Government Printing Office, 1994), p. 316.

4. Jost, "Downward Mobility," p. 629.

5. Fred Hawthorne, "Thought about Your Pension? You Will," *New York Times*, August 25, 1994, p. A24.

6. Steven Pearlstein, "Corporate Cutbacks Yet to Pay Off," *Washington Post*, January 4, 1994, p. B6.

7. Steven Pearlstein, "The Downsizing Trap," *Washington Post National Edition*, December 18, 1993, pp. 18–19.

8. Louis Uchitelle, "Moonlighting Plus: 3-Job Families Are on the Rise," *New York Times*, August 16, 1994, p. D18.

9. Tamar Lewin, "Low Pay and Closed Doors Greet Young in Job Market," *New York Times*, March 10, 1994, p. B12.

10. Sylvia Nasar, "Statistics Reveal Bulk of New Jobs Pay Over Average," *New York Times*, October 17, 1994, pp. A1, D4; George J. Church, "We're #1 and It Hurts," *Time*, October 24, 1994, pp. 51–56.

11. *The State of Working America: 1994–95* (Washington, D.C: Economic Policy Institute, 1994), pp. 165–67.

12. Church, "We're #1 and It Hurts," p.55.

13. John Byrne, "The Pain of Downsizing," *Business Week,* May 9, 1994, p. 61; G. Pascal Zachary, "Layoff Announcements Increased 39 Percent in August as Merger Activity Picked Up," *Wall Street Journal,* September 6, 1995, p. 3.

14. John Byrne, "Belt-Tightening the Smart Way," *Business Week,* October 22, 1993, pp. 34–38.

15. American Management Association, *1994 AMA Survey on Downsizing and Assistance to Dislocated Workers,* New York, July 1994, p. 3.

16. Louis Uchitelle, "Job Extinction Evolving into a Fact of Life in U.S.," *New York Times,* March 22, 1994, p. A1.

17. "Wage Gap Between Manufacturing, Service Shrinking, Economist Says," *Employment and Training Reporter,* August 3, 1994, p. 920.

18. "Low-Wage Workers Remain in Stagnant Job Market Despite Improved Economy," *Employment and Training Reporter,* June 8, 1994, p. 763.

19. The Roper Center, University of Connecticut, Storrs, Conn., Conference Board Survey, June 1994.

20. George Church, "Jobs in an Age of Insecurity," *Time,* November 22, 1993, p. 35.

21. Church, "We're #1 and it Hurts," p. 51.

22. Archival data at The Roper Center, University of Connecticut, Storrs, Conn.

23. Ibid.

24. Lewin, "Low Pay and Closed Doors Greet Young in Job Market," p. B12.

25. Jost, "Downward Mobility," p. 628.

26. The Bureau of Labor Statistics defines displaced workers as those twenty years or older with at least three years tenure who lost jobs due to plant closings or moves, the elimination of positions or shift, or slack work. See Jennifer M. Gardner, "Recession Swells County of Displaced Workers," *Monthly Labor Review,* June 1993, p. 14.

27. U.S. Department of Labor, *The Changing Labor Market and the Need for a Reemployment Response* (Washington, D.C.: U.S. Government Printing Office, December 1993), pp. 4–5.

28. Linda Levine, "Dislocated Workers: Characteristics and Experiences, 1979–1992," Congressional Research Service, November 16, 1992, CRS1-2; U.S. Department of Commerce, *Statistical Abstract of the United States, 1995* (Washington, D.C.: Government Printing Office, 1995), p. 419.

29. Bennett Harrison, *Lean and Mean: The Changing Landscape of Corporate Power in the Age of Flexibility* (New York: Basic Books, 1994).

30. U.S. Department of Commerce, Bureau of the Census, *Statistical Abstract of the United States, 1993* (Washington, D.C.: Government Printing Office, 1993), p. 410; U.S. Department of Commerce, Bureau of the Census, *Statistical Abstract of the United States, 1995* (Washington, D.C.: Government Printing Office, 1995), p. 417.

31. Levine, "Dislocated Workers: Characteristics and Experiences, 1979–1992," CRS-5.

32. "Continuing Layoffs Obscure Economic Gains and Dismay Employees," *Employment and Training Reporter*, December 1, 1993, p. 235.

33. U.S. Department of Labor, *Monthly Labor Review*, May 1991, p. 4.

34. U.S. Council of Economic Advisers, *Economic Report of the President, 1994* (Washington, D.C.: Government Printing Office, 1994), pp. 318–19.

35. "Manufacturers Will Boost Production, Not Jobs, in 1994," *Employment and Training Reporter*, January 12, 1994, p. 344.

36. "Wage Gap Between Manufacturing, Service Sector Shrinking, Economists Says," *Employment and Training Reporter*, August 3, 1994, p. 919.

37. "Wage Gap Between Manufacturing, Service Sector Shrinking, Economist Says," p. 920.

38. Council of Economic Advisers, *Economic Report of the President, 1994*, p. 107.

39. Ibid., p. 108.

40. Robert Tomasko, *Downsizing: Reshaping the Corporation for the Future* (New York: American Management Association, 1990).

41. American Management Association, *1995 AMA Survey on Downsizing and Assistance to Dislocated Workers*, p. 3.

42. "Salaried Workers Are Targets of Corporate Downsizing," *HR Focus* 71, no. 6 (June 1994): 21.

43. Kim Cameron, "Strategies for Successful Organizational Downsizing," *Human Resource Management*, Summer 1994, p. 191.

44. U.S. Department of Commerce, Bureau of the Census, *Statistical Abstract of the United States, 1988* (Washington, D.C.: Government Printing Office, 1988), p. 375.

45. U.S. Department of Labor, *Monthly Labor Review*, May 1991, p. 4.

46. U.S. Department of Defense, *National Defense Budget Estimates, Fiscal Year 1995* (Washington, D.C.: Government Printing Office, 1995), Table 7.7.

47. *Dislocation of Defense Industry Workers* (Masters thesis, Harvard University, December 1992), p. 2.

48. U.S. Department of Defense, *National Defense Estimates for FY 95*, Table 7-7.

49. Cameron, "Strategies for Successful Organizational Downsizing," p. 190.

50. American Management Association, *1993 AMA Survey on Downsizing and Assistance to Dislocated Workers*, New York, July 1993, p. 2.

51. *1994 American Marketing Association Survey on Downsizing and Assistance to Dislocated Workers,* July 1994, p. 2; *1995 American Marketing Association Survey on Downsizing and Assistance to Dislocated Workers,* July 1995, p. 2.

52. Lance Morrow, "The Temping of America," *Time*, March 29, 1993, pp. 40–47.

53. Morrow, "The Temping of America," pp. 40–47.

54. See, for example, Bennett Harrison, "The Dark Side of Flexible Production," *Technology Review*, May/June 1994, pp. 30–45; and Beverly Geber, "The Flexible Work Force: Using Contingent Workers Wisely and Humanely," *Training*, December 1993, p. 24.

55. Levin, "Low Pay and Closed Doors Greet Young in Job Market," pp. A1, B12.

56. Chris Tilly, "Reasons for the Continuing Growth of Part-time Employment," *Monthly Labor Review*, March 1991, pp. 10–11.

57. "Temps May Not Be as Cost-Effective as Many Employers Think, Prof Says," *Employment and Training Reporter*, September 1, 1993, p. 1035.

58. Harrison, "The Dark Side of Flexible Production," p. 40.

59. "New Data on Contingent and Alternative Employment Examined by BLS," Press Release on U.S. Bureau of Labor Statistics World Wide Web Homepage, August 17, 1995, stats.bls.gov/blshome.html.

60. Jost, "Downward Mobility," p. 630.

61. Morrow, "The Temping of America," pp. 40–47.

62. Peter T. Kilborn, "More Women Take Low-Wage Jobs Just so Their Families Can Get By," *New York Times*, March 13, 1994, p. A24.

63. Ann M. Thayer, "Temporary Employees Fill Niches in Chemical R&D Work Force," *Chemical and Engineering News*, vol. 72, no. 9 (February 28, 1994): 25–30.

64. Uchitelle, "Job Extinction Evolving into a Fact of Life in U.S.," p. A1.

65. Virginia du Rivage, ed., *New Policies for the Part-Time and Contingent Workforce* (Armonk, N.Y.: M.E. Sharpe, 1992), p. 45.

66. Morrow, "The Temping of America," pp. 40–47.

67. Harrison, "The Dark Side of Flexible Production," p. 45.

68. For a detailed analysis of the pressures moving companies toward continued downsizing, see Tomasko, *Downsizing: Reshaping the Corporation for the Future*, and Harrison, *Lean and Mean*.

69. The Wyatt Company, *Best Practices in Corporate Restructuring: Wyatt's 1993 Survey of Corporate Restructuring* (Chicago, Ill.: The Wyatt Company, 1993), pp. 17, 34.

70. Paul R. Krugman and Robert Z. Lawrence, "Trade, Jobs, and Wages," *Scientific American*, April 1992, pp. 44–49.

71. "Evidence Shows U.S. Jobs Displaced by Japanese Auto 'Transplants,'" *Employment and Training Reporter*, February 23, 1994, p. 458.

72. James Treece and John Hoerr, "Shaking Up Detroit," *Business Week,* August 14, 1989.

73. Internal memorandum reviewing NAFTA, Office of the United States Trade Representative, April, 1992; see also John S. McClenahen, "NAFTA after Two Years," *Industry Week,* January 8, 1996, p. 21.

74. Council of Economic Advisers, *Economic Report of the President, 1994,* p. 230.

75. Nasar, "Statistics Reveal Bulk of New Jobs Pay Over Average," p. A1.

76. Uchitelle, "Job Extinction Evolving into a Fact of Life in U.S.," p. A1.

77. U.S. Department of Commerce, *Statistical Abstract of the United States, 1993,* p. 645.

78. The Workforce Investment Strategy (AFL-CIO), Executive Summary (Draft), August 30, 1993, p. 2.

79. See, for example, Harrison, *Lean and Mean.*

80. Pearlstein, "The Downsizing Trap."

81. Kim S. Cameron, "Investigating Organizational Downsizing— Fundamental Issues," *Human Resource Management* 33, no. 2 (Summer 1994): 183.

82. William Baumol, "When Downsizing Becomes Dumbsizing," *Time,* March 15, 1993, p. 15.

83. Michelle Celarier, "Lehman on Its Own," *Global Finance* 8, no. 4 (April 1994): 19–21.

84. Cameron, "Investigating Organizational Downsizing," p. 183.

85. *Casper Star-Tribune* (Wyoming) 1993.

86. Council of Economic Advisers, *Economic Report of the President, 1995,* p. 322.

87. See Jennifer M. Gardner, "Recession Swells Count of Displaced Workers," *Monthly Labor Review*, June 1993, p. 18.

88. Cameron, "Strategies for Successful Organizational Downsizing," p. 191.

89. Gardner, "Recession Swells Count of Displaced Workers," 16.

90. "Advance Notice Doesn't Help Laid-Off Workers, BLS Finds," *Employment and Training Reporter,* September 21, 1994, p. 48.

91. Louis Jacobson, Robert LaLonde, and Daniel Sullivan, *The Costs of Worker Dislocation* (Kalamazoo, Mich.: W. E. Upjohn Institute for Employment Research, 1993), p. 137.

92. Ibid., p. 137.

93. Daniel Hamermesh, "What Do We Know about Worker Displacement in the U.S.?" *Industrial Relations* 28, no. 1 (Winter 1989): 52–53.

94. Jacobson, et al., *The Cost of Worker Dislocation*, p. 117.

95. "Advance Notice Doesn't Help Laid-Off Workers, BLS Finds," p. 49.

96. Lori G. Kletzer, "Job Displacement, 1979–86: How Blacks Fared Relative to Whites," *Monthly Labor Review*, July 1991, p. 23.

97. See Caroline Clarke, "Downsizing Trounces Diversity," *Black Enterprise* 24, no. 7 (February 1994): 69–74; and Alfred Edmond, "Gee, Blacks Really Did Lose More Jobs," *Black Enterprise* 24, no. 5 (December 1993): 20.

98. U.S. Council of Economic Advisers, *Economic Report of the President, 1994*, p. 108; see also U.S. Department of Commerce, Bureau of the Census, *Statistical Abstract of the United States, 1995,* p. 422.

99. Congressional Budget Office, *Displaced Workers; Trends in the 1980s and Implications for the Future* (Washington, D.C.: Government Printing Office, 1993), p. xiii.

100. U.S. Department of Commerce, Bureau of the Census, *Statistical Abstract of the United States, 1995*, p. 157.

101. American Management Association, *1993 AMA Survey on Downsizing and Assistance to Displaced Workers*, New York, July 1993, p. 4. The 1993 AMA Survey is a compilation of survey responses from 870 businesses on their experiences with downsizing.

102. Joseph Berger, "The Pain of Layoffs for Ex-Senior I.B.M. Workers," *New York Times*, December 22, 1993, p. B5.

103. John Portz, *The Politics of Plant Closing* (Lawrence: University Press of Kansas, 1990).

104. Benjamin Weiser, "When the Plant Closes," *Washington Post National Weekly Edition*, January 6, 1994, p. 14.

105. Robert D. Reich, "Companies Are Cutting Their Hearts Out," *New York Times Magazine*, February 7, 1994, pp. 30–31.

106. Interview with Pratt and Whitney employee in Hartford, Connecticut, October 14, 1993.

107. Weiser, "When the Plant Closes," p. 14.

108. Jost, "Downward Mobility," p. 627.

109. Kirk Johnson, "Evolution of the Workplace Alters Office Relationships," *New York Times*, October 5, 1994, p. B8.

110. Ibid., p. B1.

111. U.S. Department of Labor, *The Changing Labor Market and the Need for a Reemployment Response,* December 1993, p. 2.

112. Peter F. Drucker, *Post-Capitalist Society* (New York: Harper Business, 1993).

113. William Bridges, "The End of the Job," *Fortune,* September 19, 1994, pp. 69–74.

114. William Bridges, *Job Shift* (New York: Addison-Wesley, 1994).

115. Catherine S. Manegold, "Reich Urges Executives To Aid Labor," *New York Times,* September 25, 1994, p. A25.

116. "How Will We Live with the Tumult," *Fortune,* December 13, 1993, p. 123.

117. John Bishop, "A Program of Research on the Role of Employer Training in Ameliorating Skill Shortages and Enhancing Productivity and Competitiveness" (Philadelphia: University of Pennsylvania, Center for Educational Quality of the Workforce, 1993).

118. See, for example, Evelyn Ganzglass, ed., *Excellence at Work: Policy Options Papers for the National Governors' Association* (Kalamazoo, Mich.: W. E. Upjohn Institute for Employment Research, 1992); Paul Osterman and Rosemary Batt, "Employer-Centered Training for International Competitiveness: Lessons from State Programs," *Journal of Policy Analysis and Management* 12, no. 3, pp. 456–77.

119. See, for example, M. Bailey, G. Burtless, and R. Litan, *Growth With Equity: Economic Policy Making for the Next Century* (Washington, D.C.: The Brookings Institution, 1993); Robert Reich, *Work of Nations: Preparing Ourselves for 21st Century Capitalism* (New York: A. A. Knopf, 1991); Commission on the Skills of the American Workforce, "America's Choice: High Skill or Low Wages," Rochester, New York, National Center on Education and the Economy, 1990; Paul Osterman, *Employment Futures: Reorganization, Dislocation, and Public Policy* (New York: Oxford University Press, 1988); "The New American Workplace: A Labor Perspective," a report by the AFL-CIO Committee on the Evolution of Work, February 1994; Committee for Economic Development, *Work and Change: Labor Market Adjustment Policies in a Competitive World* (New York, 1987); and the National Association of Manufacturers, "Workforce Readiness: How to Meet Our Greatest Competitive Challenges" (Washington, D.C., December, 1992).

120. Michael E. Porter, *The Competitive Advantage of Nations* (New York: The Free Press, 1990), p. 628.

121. Peter Passell, "Economic Scene: Why Isn't a Better Economy Helping Clinton's Popularity?" *New York Times,* November 3, 1994, D2.

CHAPTER 2

1. Carrie Leana and Daniel Feldman, *Coping with Job Loss: How Individuals, Organizations and Communities Respond to Layoffs* (New York: Lexington Books, 1992), p. 122.

2. Kim S. Cameron, "Guest Editor's Note: Investigating Organizational Downsizing—Fundamental Issues," *Human Resource Management* 33, no. 2 (Summer 1994): 187.

3. American Management Association, *1994 American Management Association Survey on Downsizing and Assistance to Dislocated Workers*, New York, July 1994, p. 4.

4. National Commission for Employment Policy, *Assisting Dislocated Workers: Alternatives to Layoffs, and the Role of the Employment Service under EDWAA*, Special Report No. 30, October 1991, p. 21; see also Pamela Benz, Lisa Miedich, and Robert Whaley, "Reducing the Impact of Staff Reductions on Unemployment Costs," *Employment Relations Today*, Summer 1993, pp. 207–13.

5. Darrell. L. Browning, "No Layoff Policies," *Human Resource Executive*, June 24, 1994, pp. 54–57.

6. Barnaby J. Feder, "Recasting a Model Incentive Strategy," *New York Times*, September 5, 1994, pp. 33, 36.

7. Jay Stuller, "Why Not 'Inplacement'?" *Training*, June 1993, pp. 37–41.

8. Melina Henneberger, "Hospitals Swap Job Guarantees for Pay Limits," *New York Times*, September 26, 1994, p. A1.

9. John Byrne, "The Pain of Downsizing," *Business Week*, May 9, 1994, p. 61.

10. Leana and Feldman, *Coping with Job Loss*, p. 122.

11. Benz, Miedich, and Whaley, "Reducing the Impact of Staff Reductions on Unemployment Costs," p. 209.

12. Vernita Smith, "The Top 50: The Road Ahead. The Nation's Largest Employers Prepare for Tomorrow," *Human Resource Executive*, January 1994, p. 20.

13. John Hoerr, "Big Blues for Laid-Off IBM Work Force," *Business and Society Review*, Spring 1994, p. 39.

14. The Roper Center, *Public Attitude Monitor*, University of Connecticut, Storrs, Conn., June 6, 1992.

15. John Hoerr, "Big Blues for Laid-Off IBM Work Force," p. 39.

16. American Management Association, *1994 AMA Survey on Downsizing and Assistance to Displaced Workers*, New York, 1993. The survey was mailed to human resource managers at companies that are AMA members in July 1994. The AMA survey is not reflective of the

private sector as a whole. Only 2 percent of the nation's businesses gross $10 million annually, but 90 percent of the firm's in the AMA survey have annual sales of $10 million or more. While 20 percent of the nation's businesses are engaged in manufacturing, 46 percent of the AMA respondents are manufacturing firms. It is likely, therefore, that the AMA survey provides an optimistic picture of the degree to which individuals receive help in moving from one job to another.

17. Robert Tomasko, *Downsizing: Reshaping the Corporation for the Future* (New York: American Management Association, 1990), pp. 190–91; and Rod Willis, "What's Happening to America's Middle Managers?" *Management Review*, January 1987, p. 28.

18. Leana and Feldman, *Coping with Job Loss*, p. 116; and H. G. Kaufman, *Professionals in Search of Work: Coping with the Stress of Job Loss and Unemployment* (New York: John Wiley and Sons, 1982).

19. U.S. General Accounting Office, *Dislocated Workers: Worker Adjustment and Retraining Notification Act Not Meeting Its Goals*, Washington, D.C., February 1993, pp. 4–5.

20. "Advance Notice Doesn't Help Laid-Off Workers, BLS Finds," *Employment and Training Reporter*, September 21, 1994, p. 18.

21. U.S. Department of Labor, Title III Program Performance for Program Year 1991.

22. U.S. General Accounting Office, *Dislocated Workers*, pp. 4–5.

23. Coopers & Lybrand, *Severance Pay Update for 1993* (New York, March 1994).

24. Stephen Franklin, "Candy Firm Creates Recipe for Sweeter Plant Closing," *Chicago Tribune*, March 28, 1992, p. 1.

25. Leana and Feldman, *Coping with Job Loss*, p. 127.

26. Minda Zetlin "Can IBM Soften the Blow?" *Management Review,* August 1993, pp. 25–29.

27. A survey by Rights Associates of 1,800 firms found that nearly two-thirds provided severance payments in 1991. See Frank P. Louchbeim, "Severance Survey: What Companies Are Doing Now," *Employment Relations Today*, Spring 1991, pp. 9–14.

28. "Digital Cuts Generous Severance Package in New Round of Layoffs," *Compensation & Benefits Review*, March/April 1993, p. 14.

29. "Severance: The Corporate Response," *Personnel Journal*, July 1991, pp. 9–10.

30. Paul Williamson, "Severance Pay with a Twist," *Small Business Reports*, April 1994, p. 9.

31. Wyatt Company, *Best Practices in Corporate Restructuring: Wyatt's 1993 Survey of Corporate Restructuring* (Chicago, Ill.: The Wyatt Company, 1993), p. 4. This 1993 report is a summary of restructuring

practices of 531 firms responding to a follow-up survey from 1988 by Wyatt.

32. Leana and Feldman, *Coping with Job Loss*, p. 123.

33. See, for example, Louis Jacobson, Robert LaLonde, and Daniel Sullivan, *The Cost of Worker Dislocation* (Kalamazoo, Mich.: W. E. Upjohn Institute for Employment Research, 1993), pp. 154–56; and Duane E. Leigh, *Does Training Work for Dislocated Workers? A Survey of Existing Evidence* (Kalamazoo, Mich.: W. E. Upjohn Institute for Employment Research, 1990).

34. Stephanie Overman, "Retraining Puts Workers Back on Track," *HR Magazine*, August 1992, p. 40.

35. The analysis the follows is adapted from Daniel C. Feldman and Carrier R. Leana, "Better Practices in Managing Layoffs," *Human Resource Management* 33, no. 2 (Summer 1994): 239–40.

36. Case studies of several firms are offered in Feldman and Leana, "Better Practices in Managing Layoffs," pp. 239–60.

37. See American Management Association, *AMA Survey on Downsizing and Assistance to Displaced Workers*, 1987, 1988, 1989, 1990, 1991, 1992, 1993.

38. Kim S. Cameron, "Strategies for Successful Organizational Downsizing," *Human Resource Management* 33, no. 2 (Summer 1994): 190.

39. Aneil K. Mishra and Karen E. Mishra, "The Role of Mutual Trust in Effective Downsizing Strategies," *Human Resource Management* 33, no. 2 (Summer 1994): 263.

40. "Are You a Cost-cutting Addict?" *CA Magazine*, September 1993, p. 12.

41. "Re-engineering Review," *The Economist*, July 2, 1994, p. 66.

42. Cameron, "Strategies for Successful Organizational Downsizing," p. 206.

43. "Are You a Cost-cutting Addict?" p. 12.

44. George J. Church, "We're #1 and It Hurts," *Time*, October 24, 1994, p. 52.

45. Smith, "The Top 50: The Road Ahead," p. 23.

46. Steven Pearlstein, "The Downsizing Trap," *Washington Post National Edition*, December 18, 1993, pp. 18–19.

47. Church, "We're #1 and it Hurts," p. 54; and Lee Sullivan, "The Office That Never Closes," *Forbes* 153, no. 11 (May 23, 1994).

48. Richard Rosenberg, "Human Resource Challenges in Bank Downsizing and Mergers," *World of Banking* 12, no. 5 (September/October 1993): 11–14.

49. Houda Samaha, "Helping Survivors Stay on Track," *Human Resources Professional* 5, no. 4 (Spring 1993): 12–14.

50. Craig Eric Schneier, Douglas G. Shaw, and Richard W. Beatty, "Companies' Attempts to Improve Performance While Containing Costs: Quick Fix Versus Lasting Change," *Human Resource Planning* 15, no. 3, p. 3.

51. Samaha, "Helping Survivors Stay on Track," p. 13.

52. Ronald Henkoff, "Getting Beyond Downsizing," *Fortune*, January 10, 1994, pp. 58–64.

53. Lisa Baggerman, "The Futility of Downsizing," *Industry Week,* January 18, 1993, pp. 27–29.

54. Smith, "The Top 50: The Road Ahead," p. 23.

55. Steven Pearlstein, "Corporate Cutbacks Yet to Pay Off," *Washington Post,* January 4, 1994, p. B6.

56. Judy Quinn, "Employee Morale Is Getting Worse," *Incentive* 168, no. 1 (January 1994): 5.

57. Richard Pinola, "Building a Winning Team after a Downsizing," *Compensation and Benefits Management* 10, no. 1 (Winter 1994): 54–59.

58. Duane Tway, "The Living Breathing Organization," *Training* 30, no. 8 (August 1993): 74.

59. "Employee Trust Wanes After Cutbacks," *Employment and Training Reporter*, February 23, 1994, p. 465.

60. American Management Association, *1994 AMA Survey on Downsizing and Assistance to Displaced Workers*, New York, July 1994, p. 3.

61. Daniel J. McConville, "The Upside of Downsizing," *Industry Week*, May 17, 1993.

62. Wyatt Company, *Best Practices in Corporate Restructuring*, p. 3.

63. Robert Weisman, "Pratt Morale Way Down, Survey of Workers Finds," *Hartford Courant*, November 2, 1994, p. A7.

64. Pratt & Whitney, *Employees Concerned about Jobs, Future*, October 1993.

65. Ibid.

66. Michael Hitt, "Human Capital and Strategic Competitiveness in the 1990s," *Journal of Management Development 1994* 13, no. 1, pp. 35–46.

67. James Emshoff, "How to Increase Employee Loyalty While You Downsize," *Business Horizons* 37, no. 2 (March/April 1994): 49–57.

68. Michael Hammer and James Champy, *Reengineering the Corporation: A Manifesto for Business Revolution* (New York: Harper Business, 1993).

69. American Management Association, *1993 Survey on Downsizing and Assistance to Displaced Workers*, New York, July 1993.

70. Laurel Touby, "The Business of America Is Jobs," *Journal of Business Strategy* 14, no. 6 (November/December 1993): 20–31.

71. U.S. Department of Labor, *Monthly Labor Review*, May 1991, p. 4.

72. Aaron Bernstein, "Why America Needs Unions but Not the Kind It Has Now," *Business Week*, May 23, 1994; *Statistical Abstract of the United States, 1995*, p. 443.

73. Wayne Vroman and Douglas Wissoker, *Alternatives for Managing Production Cutbacks: A Report to the National Commission for Employment Policy* (Washington, D.C.: Government Printing Office, 1990), pp. 34–36.

74. Barry Bluestone and Irving Bluestone, *Negotiating the Future* (New York: Basic Books, 1992), p. 209.

75. The Brotherhood of Electrical Workers and Commonwealth Edison both allow part-time workers.

76. Michael Cimini, Susan Behrmann, and Eric Johnson, "Labor-Management Bargaining in 1993," *Monthly Labor Review*, January 1994, p. 20.

77. Lawrence Mishel and Paula Voos, eds., *Unions and Economic Competitiveness* (New York: M.E. Sharpe, 1991), pp. 129–134.

78. Cimini, et al., "Labor-Management Bargaining in 1993," p. 20.

79. See, for example, Feldman and Leana, "Better Practices in Managing Layoffs," pp. 248–50.

80. U.S. Department of Commerce, Bureau of the Census, *Statistical Abstract of the United States, 1995* (Washington, D.C.: Government Printing Office, 1993), p. 417.

81. William Serrin, *Homestead: The Glory and Tragedy of an American Steel Town* (New York: Times Books, 1992), p. 4.

82. United Steel Workers of America, International Headquarters Task Force, *A Summary Report on the Development and Progress of the United Steelworkers of America Dislocated Worker Assistance Program, 1983–1993: A Decade Later*, Pittsburgh, Penn., July 17, 1993, p. 14.

83. Ibid., pp. 29, 35.

84. Ibid., p. 31.

85. Ibid., p. 26.

86. Ibid., p. 3.

87. The principles are taken from ibid., pp. 34–35.

88. Telephone interview with Mr. John T. Smith, assistant to the international President, USWA, April 11, 1994.

Chapter 3

1. Aneil Mishra and Karne Mishra, "The Role of Mutual Trust in Effective Downsizing Strategies," *Human Resource Management* 33, no. 2 (Summer 1994): 269.

2. Kim S. Cameron, "Strategies for Downsizing," *Human Resource Management* 33, no. 2 (Summer 1994): 196.

3. George J. Church, "We're #1 and It Hurts," *Time*, October 24, 1994, p. 52; "General Motor's $6.9 Billion Profit Is Largest Ever," *Detroit News and Free Press*, January 31, 1996, p. A1.

4. U.S. Department of Commerce, International Trade Administration, "Motor Vehicles and Parts," in *U.S. Industrial Outlook 1994* (Washington, D.C.: Government Printing Office, 1993), pp. 35.1–35.31.

5. James Bennet, "Auto Plants Pushed to Their Limits," *New York Times*, September 24, 1994, pp. 33, 43.

6. U.S. Department of Commerce, "Motor Vehicles and Parts," p. 35.12.

7. Ibid., p. 35.2.

8. Church, "We're #1 and It Hurts," p. 52.

9. "Managing American Labor," *Financial World* 160, no. 13 (June 25, 1991): 56–62.

10. "Posturing," *Economist,* June 26, 1993, p. 73.

11. Brian S. Moskal, "Auto Talks Require Enlightenment," *Industry Week*, July 2, 1990, pp. 49–50.

12. "Contracts Describe Benefit Plans in Automobile, Steel Industries," *Employee Benefit Plan Review* 48, no. 7 (January 1994): 48–49.

13. "Developments in Industrial Relations," *Monthly Labor Review*, December 1993, p. 50.

14. David Woodruff, "The UAW Needs a Good Body Shop," *Business Week*, June 22, 1992, pp. 127–28.

15. 1992 Annual Report of the UAW/Chrysler Joint Activities Board.

16. Ibid.

17. Agreement between General Motors Corporation and the UAW, September 17, 1990, p. 226.

18. Deborah Shalowitz, "GM Offering Paid 'Job Hunt' Leave," *Business Insurance* 27, no. 9 (March 1, 1993): 6.

19. Liz Pinto, "UAW Proposes Trading Jobs for COLAs," *Pensions & Investments* 20, no. 17 (August 3, 1992): 25.

20. Agreement between General Motors Corporation and the UAW, September 17, 1990, p. 204. These provisions were retained in the 1993 round of negotiations. See "Developments in Industrial Relations," *Monthly Labor Review*, December 1993, p. 50.

21. Agreement between General Motors corporation and the UAW. September 17, 1990, p. 204.

22. "Developments in Industrial Relations," *Monthly Labor Review,* March 1994, p. 50.

23. Ibid.

24. Kim S. Cameron, "Investigating Organization Downsizing: Fundamental Issues," *Human Resource Management* 33, no. 2 (Summer 1994): 182–88; interview with Julie Kennedy, equity analyst, Goldman Sachs, April 1994.

25. Crowell, Weedon & Company, Market Analysis Report, New York, March 1994, p. 1.

26. Edmund Andrews, "AT&T Cutting Up to 15,000 Jobs to Trim Costs," *New York Times*, February 11, 1994, p. D1; Allan Sloan, "The Hitmen," *Newsweek*, February 26, 1996, p. 44.

27. Andrews, "AT&T Cutting Up to 15,000 Jobs to Trim Costs," p. D1.

28. "AT&T Cuts Likely to Send Jobs to Valley," *Arizona Republic*, August 20, 1993; and "GTE to Cut 2,600 Jobs," *St. Petersburg Times*, September 4, 1993.

29. Interview with Ed McCraw, director, Financial and Editorial Communications, GTE, March 1994.

30. *Denver Post*, September 18, 1993.

31. "MCI Confirms Overhaul: Consolidation May Affect 1,500 Workers," *Dallas Morning News*, November 16, 1990.

32. Andrews, "AT&T Cutting Up to 15,000 Jobs to Trim Costs," p. D1.

33. *Sacramento Bee*, March 10, 1993.

34. *Los Angeles Times*, September 21, 1993; *Denver Post*, September 18, 1993.

35. Interview with Ed McCraw, director, Financial and Editorial Communications, GTE.

36. Interview with Bernie Goodrich, director, public relations, MCI, March 1994.

37. Vivian Guilfroy, Teresa Parkers, Monika K. Aring, and Judy Leff, "The Teaching Firm: The Alliance for Employee Growth and Development," The Institute for Education and Employment Education Development Center, Inc., Newton, Mass., February 1994.

38. Interview with Donald Treinen, executive codirector, AT&T Alliance, Somerset, New Jersey, March 1994.

39. Eileen Appelbaum and Rosemary Batt, *The New American Workplace: Transforming Work Systems in the United States* (Ithaca, N.Y.: ILR Press, 1994), p. 113.

40. "Telecommunications: The End of the Line," *Economist*, October 23, 1993, p. 10.

41. Interview with Bernie Goodrich, director, public relations, MCI, March 1994.

42. Hedrick Smith, *The Power Game: How Washington Works* (New York: Random House, 1988), p. 190.

43. Paul Kennedy, *The Rise and Fall of the Great Powers: Economic Change and Military Conflict from 1500 to 2000* (New York: Random House, 1987), p. 522.

44. Defense Budget Project, Potential Impact of Defense Spending Reductions on the Defense Related Labor Force By State, Washington, D.C., May 1993, p. 1.

45. U.S. Department of Defense, *National Defense Estimates for Fiscal Year 1995* (Washington, D.C.: Government Printing Office, 1994), Table 7-7.

46. U.S. Department of Commerce, Bureau of the Census, *Statistical Abstract of the United States, 1993* (Washington, D.C.: Government Printing Office, 1993), p. 410.

47. Defense Budget Project, "Potential Impact of Defense Spending Reductions on the Defense Related Labor Force By State," p. 12.

48. Joyce Reimherr, "A Comparison of Four Policy Approaches to the Dislocation of Defense Industry Workers," (masters thesis, Howard University, 1992).

49. House Armed Services Committee, February 19, 1992.

50. Ibid.

51. Ibid.

52. Louis Uchitelle, "Job Extinction Evolving into a Fact of Life in U.S.," *New York Times*, March 22, 1994.

53. Defense Budget Project, "Potential Impact of Defense Spending Reductions on the Defense Related Labor Force by State," pp. 11, 22.

54. Ibid., p. 11.

55. Ibid.

56. Ibid.

57. Ibid., p. 12.

58. Interview with Patricia DeMeco, Human Resources Manager, Philadelphia Naval Yard, March 9, 1994.

59. Interview with Howard Rowe, Human Resources Manager, Martin Marietta Corporation, Colorado Springs, Colorado, March 25, 1994.

60. Interview with Senior Manager, Martin Marietta, March 22, 1994.

61. Ibid.

62. Interview with Patricia DeMeco, March 22, 1994.

63. "Federal Efforts Fail Defense Workers in St. Louis, Report Says," *Employment and Training Reporter*, January 25, 1994, p. 389.

64. Interview with William Zimbrusky, Human Resources Manager, Electric Boat Division, General Dynamic Corporation, Groton, Connecticut, March 23, 1994.

65. Defense Budget Project, "Potential Impact of Defense Spending Reductions on the Defense Related Labor Force By State," p. 12.

66. "Broad Impact Seen From Defense Cuts," *Employment and Training Reporter*, May 6, 1993, p. 676.

CHAPTER 4

1. "Trade Adjustment Assistance: The Program for Workers," Congressional Research Service Report, September 17, 1993, p. 1.

2. Testimony presented before the U.S. Congress, House Subcommittee on Employment, Housing and Aviation, Committee on Government

Operations, *Dislocated Workers: Trade Adjustment Assistance Program Flawed*, 103d Cong., 1st sess., October 19, 1993, p. 1.

3. U.S. Congress, *National Defense Authorization Act for Fiscal Year 1995,* 103d Cong., 2d sess., 1994, Report 103–499.

4. Congressional Research Service Report, *Defense Economic Adjustment and Conversion Legislation in the 102d Congress*, March 14, 1991, p. 2.

5. Congressional Budget Office, *Reemploying Defense Workers: Current Experiences and Policy Alternatives* (Washington, D.C.: Government Printing Office, 1992), p. 5.

6. Congressional Budget Office, *The Technology Reinvestment Project: Integrating Military and Civilian Industries* (Washington, D.C.: Government Printing Office, 1992), p. 11.

7. Office of Management and Budget, *United States Budget, Fiscal Year 1993* (Washington, D.C.: Government Printing Office, 1992), p. 341.

8. James R. Storey, *Unemployment Compensation and Proposals for Reform*, Congressional Research Service Issue Brief, February 1, 1994.

9. U.S. House of Representatives, *FY 1991 Defense Authorization Act Convergence Act*, 101st Cong., 2d sess., 1990, House Report 101-923, p. 382.

10. Ibid., p. 771.

11. *Defense Industry in Transition: Issues and Options for Congress*, Congressional Research Service Issue Brief, February 15, 1992, p. 3.

12. Congressional Budget Office, *The Technology Reinvestment Project*, p. 8.

13. *Job Training Legislation and Budget Issues,* Congressional Research Service Issue Brief, March 14, 1994, p. 4.

14. Storey, "Unemployment Compensation: Proposals for Reform," p. 1.

15. Ann M. Lorderman and James R. Storey, *Adjustment Assistance for Workers Dislocated by the North American Free Trade Agreement*, Congressional Research Service, January 25, 1994.

16. Because discretionary NAFTA funding is funneled through EDWAA, the application process is nearly indistinguishable from EDWAA.

17. Testimony presented before the U.S. Congress, House Subcommittee on Employment, Housing and Aviation, Committee on Government Operations, *Dislocated Workers: Trade Adjustment Assistance Program Flawed*, 103d Cong., 1st sess., October 19, 1993, p. 7.

18. John T. Ward, "Retraining Ropes Not Always Easy to Climb," *Asbury Park Press*, February 14, 1994, p. D6.

19. Ibid., p. D16.

20. Testimony of Clarence C. Crawford, before the U.S. Congress, House Subcommittee on Employment, Housing and Aviation, Committee on Government Operations, *Multiple Employment Training Programs: Major Overhaul Needed*, 103d Cong., 2d sess., March 3, 1994, p. 3.

21. James R. Storey, *Trade Adjustment Assistance: The Program for Workers*, Congressional Research Service, September 22, 1993, p. 5.

22. Ann M. Lordeman, *Training for Dislocated Workers under the Job Training Partnership Act*, Congressional Research Service, December 3, 1992, p. 6.

23. Program performance information is only available for unemployment insurance, EDWAA, and TAA. The other programs have not been in operation long enough for the government or other groups to collect detailed information for purposes of evaluation.

24. U.S. Council of Economic Advisers, *Economic Indicators*, April 1990, 1994, p. 12.

25. Bureau of Labor Statistics, *Monthly Labor Review*, September 1995, p. 80.

26. U.S. Council of Economic Advisers, *Economic Report of the President 1995* (Washington, D.C.: Government Printing Office, 1995), p. 323.

27. Saul J. Blaustein, *Unemployment Insurance in the United States*, (Kalamazoo, Mich.: W. E. Upjohn Institute for Employment Research, 1993), p. 33.

28. "Docking the Unemployed," *Fortune*, November 13, 1993, p. 28.

29. U.S. Department of Labor, *An Examination of Declining UI Claims During the 1980s: Draft Final Report* (Washington, D.C.: Government Printing Office, 1990), p. 21.

30. Ibid., p. 24.

31. Ibid., pp. 26–30.

32. Ibid., p. 34.

33. The data reported here are from the U.S. Department of Labor, Title III program report for program year 1993, which runs through June 30, 1993. It is the last year for which data are available. Federal regulations require states to ensure that such surveys are carried out and reach at least 70 percent of program participants. Eight questions are asked of program completers in every state-based survey: Did you work for pay during the reference week (thirteenth week after program termination)? If yes, how many hours did you work during that week? What was your pay rate during that week? Did you earn any extra wages during that week in overtime, tips, bonuses? How many weeks in the entire thirteen-week period did you work for pay? Are you still with the same employer? If no, did you work at all during the thirteen-week period? How many weeks did you work?

34. Tom Redburn, "Signs of Life After Pan Am: Thousands of Workers Stranded by Airline's Sudden Demise Find Training and Jobs," *New York Times*, June 7, 1994, p. B1.

35. Timothy Egan, "Oregon, Foiling Forecasters, Thrives as It Protects Owls," *New York Times*, October 11, 1994, p. A19.

36. The states and years covered are as follows: New Jersey (1991–92), Idaho (1989–93), South Carolina (1991–92), Rhode Island (1991–92), Massachusetts (1992–93), and Washington (1990, 1992–93). The data were obtained from the states through a survey research contractor. The analysis was carried out by graduate students enrolled in the public policy program at the Eagleton Institute of Politics, Rutgers University.

37. Some of the problems of the data must be cited. The six states did not use uniform survey techniques or questionnaires. There is no way of knowing if the reported cases are representative of the universe of survey respondents, let alone of all EDWAA participants. Important information, such as whether the participant receives other government aid, is also missing. Data exist for only those people who completed training and were terminated from the program. Not taken into consideration are people who qualified for training but did not receive it, nor those who began training but did not complete it. Such self-selection among program-eligible displaced workers undermines the ability to generalize from the data. And we cannot examine how the program may have contributed to excluding certain people or preventing them from completing it.

38. For the purposes of this analysis, a full-time job was defined as working thirty-five or more hours per week. When discussing EDWAA, the U.S. Department of Labor defines a full-time job as twenty or more hours per week.

39. Unless otherwise noted, the observations about TAA are taken from a report prepared by Walter Corson, Paul Decker, Phillip Gleason, and Walter Nicholson, *International Trade and Worker Dislocations: Evaluation of the Trade Adjustment Assistance Program*, prepared by Mathematica Policy Research, Princeton, New Jersey, April 1993.

40. See, for example, testimony by Linda G. Morra before the U.S. Congress, House Subcommittee on Employment, Housing, and Aviation, Committee on Government Operations, *Dislocated Workers: Trade Adjustment Assistance Program Flawed*, 103d Cong., 1st sess., October 19, 1993.

41. Raju Narisetti, "Not Everybody Wins," *Wall Street Journal*, October 28, 1994, p. R10.

42. The cost depends on the weekly benefit, how long the benefits are received, and the share the employer pays through higher UI taxes. The weekly benefits average about 35 percent of weekly wages. Most people

get benefits for fourteen weeks. The typical employer bears about 60 percent of the cost of benefits paid to laid-off workers, though many employers are already paying the maximum UI tax rate and, as a result, suffer no punitive increase if they lay off additional workers.

CHAPTER 5

1. Information about state-funded programs is derived from a survey of administrators conducted from March through May of 1994 by the Eagleton Institute of Politics, Rutgers University. Although other studies have reported that up to forty-four states operate training programs, I have excluded programs that are not targeted at the long-term unemployed or dislocated workers. See, for example, Peter A. Creticos, Steve Duscha, and Robert G. Sheets, *State Financed, Customized Training Programs: A Comprehensive State Survey*, Report Submitted to the Office of Technology Assessment, U.S. Congress, DeKalb, Illinois, September 30, 1990.

2. Congressional Budget Office, *Displaced Workers: Trends in the 1980s and Implications for the Future* (Washington, D.C.: Government Printing Office, 1993), p. xiv.

3. Richard Swell, Deputy Director, Indiana Employment and Training Program, memorandum to Indiana Employment and Training Commission, January 31, 1991.

4. Information on the Washington Program comes from *Implementation of ESHB 1988*, a report prepared for the Washington State House Appropriations Committee, January 4, 1994.

5. Employment and Training Panel Regulations, California Code of Regulations, Title 22, Article 2, May 1993.

6. All information reported on the Workforce Development Partnership Program comes from New Jersey Employment and Training Commission, *First Annual Assessment Report of the Workforce Development Partnership Program*, Trenton, New Jersey, December 1993.

7. California Employment and Training Panel, *Annual Report 1992–93*, Sacramento, Calif., p. 5.

8. California Employment and Training Panel, *Annual Report 1992–93*, p. 20.

9. Duane E. Leigh, *Does Training Work for Displaced Workers?* (Kalamazoo, Mich.: W. E. Upjohn Institute for Employment Research, 1990), p. 58.

10. Paul Osterman and Rosemary Batt, "Employer-Centered Training for International Competitiveness: Lessons from State Programs," *Journal of Policy Analysis and Management* 12, no. 3., p. 462.

11. Peter A. Creticos and Robert G. Sheets, *Evaluating State-Financed Workplace-Based Retraining Programs: A Report on the Feasibility of a Business Screening and Performance Outcome Evaluation System* (Washington, D.C.: National Commission for Employment Policy, 1990), pp. 6–8.

12. California Employment and Training Panel, *Annual Report, 1992–93*, p. 32.

13. John T. Addison and Pedro Portugal, "Advance Notice," in John T. Addison, ed., *Job Displacement: Consequences and Implications for Policy* (Detroit, Mich.: Wayne State University Press, 1991), pp. 203–43.

14. Ronald Green, William Carmell, and Jerrold Goldberg, *1993 State by State Guide to Human Resources Law* (New York: Panel Publication, 1992), pp. 120–25.

15. Addison and Portugal, "Advance Notice," p. 208.

16. Green, et al., *1993 State by State Guide to Human Resources Law*, pp. 120–25.

17. Ibid.

18. Ibid.

19. Osterman and Batt, "Employer-Centered Training for International Competitiveness," pp. 456–77.

20. Criticos and Sheets, *Evaluating State-Financed, Workplace-Based Retraining Programs*, p. vi.

Index

199

ABOUT THE AUTHOR

Carl E. Van Horn is professor of public policy and political science at the Eagleton Institute of Politics and chair of the Department of Public Policy at the Bloustein School of Planning and Public Policy at Rutgers University. He has also taught at Georgetown University, the State University of New York at Stony Brook, and Ohio State University. In 1996, he participated in the White House Conference on Corporate Citizenship and was appointed by President Bill Clinton to a Presidential Emergency Board to investigate and mediate disputes between labor and management in the railroad industry. He has served as director of policy for the State of New Jersey in the office of Governor James Florio and on the professional staff of the Joint Economic Committee of the U.S. Congress. He is the author of several books about public policy and politics, including, most recently, *The State of the States* (CQ Press, 1996).